GETTING ON THE MONEYTRACK

Rob Black

Foreword by Pam Krueger

WILEY

John Wiley & Sons, Inc.

Published by John Wiley & Sons, Inc., Hoboken, New Jersey
Published simultaneously in Canada

For general information on our other products and services or for technical support, please contact our Customer Care Department within the United States at (800) 762-2974, outside the United States at (317) 572-3993 or fax (317) 572-4002.

Wiley also publishes its books in a variety of electronic formats. Some content that appears in print may not be available in electronic books. For more information about Wiley products, visit our web site at www.wiley.com.

Library of Congress Cataloguing-in-Publication Data:

Black, Rob.
    Getting on the moneytrack / Rob Black; with a foreword by Pam Krueger.
      p.   cm.
    ISBN-13 978-0-471-77079-4 (pbk.)
    ISBN-10 0-471-77079-5 (pbk.)
    1. Finance, Personal.   2. Investments.   I. Title.
    HG179.B516   2005
    332.024—dc22

                                                    2005020699

Printed in the United States of America

10 9 8 7 6 5 4 3 2 1

Contents

Foreword

When I was making my living as a stockbroker, about 20 or so years ago, I used to sit down face-to-face with clients or prospective clients and I'd listen as they shared their greatest hopes or their biggest fears about investing. I decided there are three types of people when it comes to money, and I developed this little habit of mentally placing each personality into one of the three categories.

The first type—call them Type A's—were the players. These were the clients who knew just enough about how the market works to be dangerously active investors. These guys didn't invest, they "took positions" in stocks and loved the drama of the market. As my clients, they called the shots. As their broker, it was my job to execute the trades as fast as possible then report the results. (Don't forget, back then, there was no Internet!) The concept of long-term investing or, God forbid, planning for specific goals was downright uncool. Type A investors were the original amateur day traders. Problem is, across the board, just like the high tech daytraders of the 1990s, the hyper vigilants bet the farm and not only lost money, but often wives and kids in the process.

The next category of client was the Type B. More often than not, Type Bs were women who for some reason were convinced they had no possible reason to be entangled with their own money, and investing was just way too complicated for them. Many times, the Type Bs became my clients because they inherited a portfolio of stocks, bonds, and/or real estate from a deceased relative or more often from a divorce settlement. It didn't really matter, because Type Bs were determined to hand

over all their decisions and their power to somebody else, ostensibly somebody much more qualified, who would also care much more deeply than they could about their own money. The Type Bs were convinced their broker would make them rich or richer and then they could get on with their shopping. Sometimes they got lucky, but most often, the daydream usually ended with a rude wake up call.

The third category, the Type Cs, were the success stories. They were clients who were willing to ask questions in order to learn what it takes to build wealth over a lifetime. Type Cs had reasonable expectations. They were not willing to give anybody else the right to make investment decisions for them. At the same time, they also recognized that they didn't have all the answers. What Type Cs wanted was a good clear understanding of what it takes to be a successful investor.

In my opinion, over the last 20 years, not much has changed. The Type Cs still make the best investors. The brokerage industry still thrives on the Type As and Bs, who operate on either greed or fear, because that's where brokers make most of their money.

What has changed is that Wall Street now intersects Main Street, thanks to the Internet. For those people seeking a clear understanding of the basics, there has never been a better time than now to take full advantage of what Wall Street has to offer. Over the past ten years, valuable investment research that was once unavailable to the average small investor is totally accessible online, often for free. Anybody can sit down at a laptop and within two minutes, sort through literally thousands of mutual funds in order to harvest the best performers. Exchange traded funds, index funds, and 401(k)s, have simplified the process to the point where you have instant diversification at the lowest possible cost. We can no longer claim that investing is too complicated. It is no more complicated than figuring out how to take advantage of the latest mortgage loans, or how to juggle six different credit cards. As a society, we have managed to become experts at borrowing money.

The financial industry would like you to believe you cannot build wealth on your own. We're here to tell you that you can if you want to. Investing is the easy part. It is the discipline to make the right investment moves that remains the biggest challenge.

This book is going to tell you the truth. *Money Track* is a PBS Television series about getting educated about your finances. Our team will tell you how to get to retirement sensibly while living well at the same time. Being educated about money means knowing how to think about money and making the right decisions for yourself without getting fleeced.

Pam Krueger
San Francisco, CA
July, 2005

GETTING 1 STARTED

HOW TO GET AND STAY ON TRACK

Most Americans want to be doing more to organize their financial affairs. Unfortunately, most of us barely have enough time to pay bills and balance the checkbook, let alone take a more organized approach to money matters. As cliché as it sounds, the first step is getting organized.

Get Organized

First, organize a routine of financial tasks. Second and perhaps most important, organize your essential financial information. Organization will not only make your life easier but will also assist your loved ones who might be asked to assess your financial picture in a worst-case scenario, should something happen to you. Keep in mind that the organization should ideally be a shared task. Far too often, there is only one person in the relationship who knows what and where the financial information is.

Organizing your financial affairs won't be exciting (and yes, some might even say dull). But that doesn't mean that it has to be a daunting and formidable task. Having a good system is the key.

Attacking the Beast:
Start with a Basic System

Do you have nameless stacks of statements, mail, and who knows what else all around the house? It's time to deal with them! Here's how to conquer the clutter.

Gather all the piles of papers and sort them into categories:

- Bills Due
- Important/Keep
- Toss/Shred

Now you can have a little fun. Buy colorful folders and label them for each household expense or activity. Buy a file cabinet or, at the very least, an accordion file holder to store your new system. (When you are getting financially organized, colorful folders and accordion files are about as much fun as you can have!)

Bills Due. Create one or two files for unpaid bills. As the bills come in, open them, clip the statement to the return envelope, and place them in the Bills Due file. Some families create two Bills Due files: one for the first pay period of the month and another for the second pay period. Use whichever system works best for you, but make a system and stick with it.

On a side note, make sure that you pay your bills on time. Missing payments can tarnish your credit rating. A ding on your credit rating can mean higher costs when borrowing in the future. If you are forced to pay more for a car or mortgage loan because of bad credit, that can mean the difference between successful financial planning and barely making ends meet.

Important/Keep. This folder is for essential household information such as receipts and warranties. Photocopy your credit cards, health cards, gym memberships, and any other cards containing important information so that if you lose your wallet, all account numbers are easily accessible and the cards are easily replaced. If you can, buy a fireproof box or get a safety deposit box in which to keep your valuable papers such as insurance policies and passports. It is also wise to keep three to five years of bank statements and credit card statements (provided you aren't paying these bills online; for more information, see the section regarding online bill paying later in this chapter.)

Toss/Shred. Anything else can now be shredded. Stay on top of this system every time you bring mail into the house. Looking for misplaced documents is stressful and not much fun. Identity theft is a huge problem so please insure yourself against the identity theft nightmare by buying a paper shredder.

The system I've described is quite simple, but you can add to it as you wish. For instance, one thing I have added is a financial binder. My binder tabs include:

- Essential personal papers: Marriage licenses, divorce papers, birth certificates, adoption papers, and Social Security information.
- Sources of income: Employment or business revenue.
- Financial assets.
- Deeds and titles: Copies of my home, automobile, and other deeded assets.
- Insurance policies: Life insurance, disability, long-term care, automobile policies.
- Employer provided benefits: Health insurance cards, disability plan, life insurance policy, etc.
- Mortgages, loans, and other liabilities: Mortgage and other substantial loans such as automobile and student loans.
- Wills, trusts, and other documents.
- Advisors/Contractors: Attorneys, stockbrokers, financial planner, insurance broker, accountant, physicians, religious leader, banker, trust officer, and so forth.
- Executor instructions: Specific funeral and obituary information as well as any other instructions you would like to pass on to your executor.
- Other

PAYING BILLS ONLINE

There are two key advantages to paying your bills online.

- It helps keep you organized by eliminating paper clutter.
- It offers electronic statements for easy viewing and account maintenance.

As discussed earlier, keeping paper clutter tamed is the secret to staying organized. Maintaining your bills, filing, and shredding will enable you to stay on top of your financial matters. You'll know where your money is going and where it needs to be. You'll develop confidence in managing your money—and you will be able to make better decisions as a result.

EMERGENCY FUNDS

Everyone should have money set aside in case of an emergency. Having a healthy emergency fund helps avoid negative financial activity, such as building credit card debt or borrowing against the house. The purpose of an emergency fund is to have cash available when the unexpected happens, such as when the clothes dryer breaks down or when a huge medical bill isn't covered by your healthcare insurance. When major life events hit, an emergency fund can be the difference between sinking or swimming financially.

Top Priority

Question: Which should come first—paying off credit card debt or setting up an emergency fund? Easy. Pay off any credit card debt on which you are paying interest of between 9 percent and 20 percent. It makes good financial sense to rid yourself of this debt first, versus earning only 1 percent to 2 percent on cash in a savings account that you are storing for an emergency.

Here's a hot tip! As soon as you pay off the credit card debt, the very next month—DO NOT DELAY!—you should continue to "sock away those monthly payments" by putting them into a savings account and building up an emergency fund. I know it sounds easy and I assure you that it is if you are disciplined and can stick to your good plan.

How Much is Enough for the Emergency Fund?

How much money should be in an emergency fund? That depends. The amount will depend on how well you have covered your other financial liabilities. How many children you have? Does the spouse work? What about stability of income, and access to low-cost loans? These are all factors to consider.

Conventional wisdom says you should have three to six months of expenses available in your emergency fund. Three to six months of emergency cash is fine when your income is good and the economic outlook is solid. But when things get a bit rougher in the economy, then it makes sense to increase this number a bit. When things get tough, people make decisions based on fear or panic. Decisions made under stress are usually not good ones. In tough times, you might tap into a 401(k) plan in order to pay for a dental bill; you will have a healthy tooth but you'll be left with a diminished retirement plan. If you eliminate greed, fear, and panic you will be better off than most who are planning their financial futures.

Keep your emergency fund in a savings account that is FDIC insured and earns little interest. Remember, this is supposed to be liquid money. Liquid money means you can access it fast when you need it. Illiquid money might be a house or a stock investment where you might have to wait for conditions to improve in order to extract your cash. As you accumulate your emergency money, you can shop around for higher rates. A great Internet resource for rate shopping is bankrate.com. You may want to consider certificates of deposit (CDs). But remember that if you need the money before the CD matures, you will pay a penalty—typically three to six months' interest.

What's an Emergency?

When you are in the midst of a true emergency there is no question you are having one. Major life changes, life-threatening situations, and legal issues all constitute an emergency, the exception being, of course, your wedding. Big-ticket items (stereos, cars, boats, TVs, etc.) and "I need a vacation" are not true emergencies either. Your emergency reserve is a fund to be taken seriously; this money should be spent only when you are in absolutely, positively, no-doubt-in-your-mind dire straits.

SMART COUPLES AND MONEY 2

LOVE AND MONEY

Preventing and overcoming money problems takes honest communication. It also takes time and effort and perhaps it even requires getting over the cliché that talking about money is like getting wisdom teeth pulled. For most people, talking about money is difficult and stressful. It involves more than just discussing the amount of income; couples must determine who is spending what and how much things cost.

Think about money for a minute—what does it mean to you? For some, it means power. To others it may mean security or status. Take some time and find out just what you and your spouse think and feel about money.

Don't wait until a problem occurs; try to talk on a regular basis, before conflicts arise. Choose a place where you won't be interrupted. I suggest taking an evening and quizzing each other about each person's views on money and their parents' views about money. Be sure to talk about things like retirement, college costs, and so forth.

You don't have to watch Dr. Phil to realize that, in general, people are more supportive of decisions when they have been allowed input. Try taking the democratic approach; be a team. Include all family members, even children, in helping make decisions about money. Let everyone have a chance to express their opinions. You will find that family members are more likely to be satisfied with the outcome if they had a hand in making the decision. Remember that we are all different in our approaches to money and none of us is right per se. There is nothing wrong with being conservative and saving in a less risky manner, nor is there anything wrong with exposing your assets to *some* volatility. There is something wrong with not addressing your retirement at all.

Clearly identify various issues or concerns. What, specifically, are the problems? None of us are immune to problems. Some families may just have more or different ones. Is the problem spending too much money, spending at the wrong time, or spending on unnecessary or unimportant items? Often financial problems are exacerbated by addiction (ex: drugs, alcohol, gambling, etc.) If you suspect this might be the cause of the problem, seek help from a local counselor or other qualified professional.

Every family member should feel free to state his or her feelings, wants, and needs freely. Others should not interject judgment or criticism. Talk about the present, and try using "I" messages instead of "you always" or "you never." For example: Instead of saying, "Why can't you ever fill the gas tank?" try saying, "I get really upset when I find the gas tank is on empty when I go to drive the car."

Be willing to negotiate toward a realistic settlement of differences. Families must be ready to compromise. A verbal agreement is fine, but a written agreement may help to avoid even more conflicts. For example, write a family contract that states: When the gas tank gets to one quarter empty, the person driving is responsible for filling the tank.

Solving family disputes this way is not only healthy, but it can also be fun. You don't have to dread talking about money. Write up colorful family contracts and have both parents and children sign them. When it comes to money matters, everyone in the tribe can literally be on the same page! One cautionary note: Nothing should ever be set in stone—leave room for adjustments, should they prove necessary. Clearly, your contracts are only a plan, but at least they will help you to communicate about important issues in your future.

THE NOTION THAT MONEY LEADS TO DIVORCE

Dr. Phil likes to simplify problem solving by making lists, so in that spirit, we'll make our own lists. It is well known that money is the biggest cause of divorce in the United States. Study the following list to determine ways to improve both the way you handle money and your relationship:

Six Steps to Prevent Divorce over Money
1. Pay all your bills on time.
2. Don't increase your debts without your partner's approval.
3. Save regularly and consistently.
4. Plan for big-ticket purchases and vacations (no buying on a whim!).
5. Talk openly about family financial matters.
6. Don't blame one another for failures in implementing steps 1 through 5.

And now for a "Top Ten" list:

Top Ten Financial Considerations for Couples
1. From the beginning, save 15 to 20 percent of your income. By combining households, you should reduce your expenses considerably, which should allow you to save. You should build your cash reserves, in both your 401k plans and in a mutual fund.
2. Rather than keeping two checkbooks as you did before you were married, pool your money into one checkbook and one savings account or money market. Getting things simplified is part of getting your financial matters organized.
3. Change all of the beneficiaries on life insurance plans, retirement plans, IRAs, and other plans to your spouse. There have been too many instances where someone forgets to update their paperwork and when they pass away an ex-girlfriend or ex-wife ends up receiving assets not truly intended for them.
4. Decide how debts accumulated by each individual prior to the marriage (i.e., student loans) will be handled. Honesty is key

here, so make sure you come clean and tell your partner about both your assets and your liabilities.

5. Work together on budgeting and tracking expenditures. This may be boring and unsexy, but it's good for the future of your relationship.

6. Discuss your approaches to handling money—is one person a spender and one a saver? Create some ground rules on handling any differences.

7. If both incomes are needed to pay expenses, be sure to carry adequate life insurance on both earners. One side note: I tend to like term life insurance because you can determine the length of time that you need to draw on the insurance in a worst-case scenario. The word "term" in term life insurance is geared to how many years you will need the insurance. I tend to recommend a 20-year term, as that is an adequate period of time in which your spouse or child can build assets to replace the need for the insurance.

8. Be sure to let each other know where important documents are kept. Personal note: My father passed away with $60,000 of credit card debt and an unsigned life insurance policy. Had my mother known about either, a better financial plan could have been crafted so as to not to leave her in a bad situation.

9. Consolidate your credit cards to avoid carrying more credit than you need. Seriously take stock of how much credit you actually *do* need. The answer may be none, or at least very little. Make your life easier. There is no need to have a wallet full of credit cards as a status symbol or just to fulfill some quota in your head.

10. Together, make a list of upcoming purchases and prioritize them. Always decide jointly how to spend your money.

If you can follow this list, then you are well on the way to both monetary and matrimonial bliss.

MONEY IS A FAMILY AFFAIR

People would rather talk about politics or even sex before they discuss money matters. For example, have you and your spouse discussed money and how it relates to your aging parents?

- Is their retirement strong and their healthcare secure?
- Do they pay their insurance on time?
- Is there an inheritance?
- Do they have a will or estate plan?

If you don't have an answer to these questions, then you might be in store for an unpleasant surprise. Secrets and money don't mix.

PARENTS WHO KEEP MONEY SECRETS FROM THEIR CHILDREN WILL:

- Unnecessarily complicate a child's financial future. Example: A grandparent might leave money to a grandchild for college, but without that knowledge, the child's parents could be saving incorrectly and focusing too much on their child's college savings plan. The opposite is also true: If the child's parents *assume* that the grandparents will chip in for college, but they never have a discussion about it, it could be financially disastrous when the money is not forthcoming. Talk to each other.
- Wreak havoc among surviving siblings. Example: The parents leave the house to their three children so upon the death of the second parent, it is divided into thirds among the kids. Two of the children want to keep the house and one wants to sell it. Resentment grows. This is more common than you might think.
- Divide the surviving family. Example: Parents assume their kids love each other and so they bequeath their assets equally, but not specifically, in the children's names. The problem occurs when the children's spouses get involved and everyone has different views about money and property. Plan your survivors' inheritance carefully. An estate plan that is not carefully thought out and precisely worded can create fuel for a nasty fire. Fighting over money can cause family—spouses, siblings, everybody—to turn on each other.

One solution might be to tell your parents to liquidate all their hard assets at death and split the proceeds equally. If there are sentimental or personal items that cannot be shared, talk it through *before* your parents are gone. Personal note: I asked my mother for her cast iron skillet and her rocking chair. She gave them to me on the spot and now there won't be any hard feelings between me and my siblings about who she promised what to.

It is your family duty to know your parents' financial situation and even your spouse's parents' financial situation. One asset all parents should pass on to their children is communication about money. Open communication creates understanding. When intent is misunderstood, nerves get frayed. Knowledge is a good thing. Learning to talk to your spouse about your parents' and his or her parents' money is invaluable to your relationship.

DEBT

Debt is not the boogeyman, as some financial experts might lead you to believe. There is no doubt that when handled poorly, debt can be a nightmare. Debt can even ruin your financial life. But it can also increase your quality of life and enable you to purchase goods more cheaply than others. Using your credit card can increase your quality of life via free air miles, hotel nights, and even 10% off on purchases at Banana Republic (or other retail stores). One can also get a certain amount of extra protection on one's purchases with a credit card. For example, a HSBC card insures you for lost baggage and damages by theft or fire. The trick is to employ debt management and make sure you have the ability to service your debt.

Perhaps it would be best to begin with a definition of debt.

A debt is a liability or obligation owed to another person or persons and required to be paid by a specified date (maturity). There are two kinds of debt: bad debt and good debt.

Good debt, such as mortgages and student loans, offers a tax deduction for the interest paid and often is used to buy an appreciating asset like a home or business. Often, good debt has low interest and is designed to be paid off over a long period of time which gives the borrower a prime opportunity to establish a favorable credit score. Good debt also leads to good things. A college degree (financed via student loans) will get you a better quality of life, higher income, and a prolonged life more often than not. A home (purchased using mortgage debt) will likely grow in value over time.

Generally speaking, most other debt is bad debt. High interest credit cards, lines of credit at department stores, and bad car leases all qualify as bad debt. When it comes to bad debt, most people don't know how much is too much and that leads to problems. Credit card debt is usually associated with retail purchases that lose value from the get go and create no lasting value.

ADVANTAGES OF DEBT

Liquidity

A line of credit sometimes can be used to reduce the need for a high balance in liquid assets or in the emergency fund. For example, if you have two months of living expenses in your emergency fund instead of the six that you might need, an established line of credit can make up the difference in case of an emergency.

Increased FICO Scores

Having a credit card that you pay off on a timely basis actually boosts your credit scores, but be sure to use a card with a low interest rate. Remember, the higher your credit score the less your borrowing costs in the future will be.

Leverage

Debt, when used properly, can leverage your purchasing power and magnify the return on investment. Example: Let's say you buy a home for $300,000. You put down $60,000 and borrow the remaining $240,000. Several years later, you sell the house for $360,000.

That's a gain of $60,000 or a 100 percent return on your investment. If you had paid for the house in cash, your gain would still be $60,000 but with an outlay of $300,000, your return would only be 20 percent.

DISADVANTAGES OF DEBT

Downward Leverage

When used inappropriately, debt can downwardly leverage or magnify losses. A perfect example of this is the same house in the previous example that you bought for $300,000. Let's say that you put $60,000 down on the $300,000 and two years later you lose your job. You can't make the payments on the home anymore so you decide to sell. The problem is that interest rates are higher than when you purchased the house and this has caused the house to lose 10 percent in value over the past two years. Therefore, you can only sell the home for $270,000, thus losing 50 percent of your down payment of $60,000.

Things Change

When you borrow, you assume that today's salary will continue (or increase) and that you will be able to repay the amounts you borrow. However, if life teaches us anything, it is that we should never assume (remember the old adage that assumptions are what makes an "ass out of you and me"?). You may discover that you want to change careers, or your job may be eliminated. If you have significant debts, you may be unable to adapt easily to these lifestyle changes.

Interest

Debt is not free money even though sometimes it may feel that way. There is always a price to pay in order to get your hands on other people's money. Even if the interest is tax-deductible, it's still an expense. If you are in a lower tax bracket, every dollar of interest is worth only a 10 cent to 15 cent reduction in taxes. It is not wise to "buy more house" simply because you think you will save more on taxes, no matter what tax bracket you are in.

BAD DEBT ISSUES

The medical bills from last year's visit to the emergency room. The second mortgage you took out four years ago. The money you borrowed from your parents that is still being held over your head years later. Imagine that this is your debt history.

Managing debt can be the most frustrating part of getting your financial act together. You might try trimming your cost of living to the bare bones and still never be able to get ahead.

When debt becomes pervasive and lowers your quality of life, consider seeing a debt specialist such as a consumer credit counselor. Too much debt can happen to anyone at any time, regardless of income level. (I bought Bobby Brown CDs in college with a credit card and little to no means of paying back that debt.) Don't be ashamed to have bad debt—only be ashamed if you choose to do nothing about it.

HOW BAD DEBT SWEPT THE LAND

For millions of Americans, debt has become a way of life. Owing thousands of dollars in high-interest debt has become the norm in this country. This is astonishing and shows that we are a nation of spenders and not savers. In fact, more than 80 million Americans now owe money on a credit card. And not just a little bit of money: The average family carrying a balance now owes more than two months of income on their credit cards. Because bankruptcy laws in the United States were recently changed, getting away from credit card debt is going to be even tougher than in the past.

You might have heard this from your grandparents: "Back in the day, if we couldn't pay cash, we didn't buy it." That was pretty much the truth: Debt just wasn't a routine part of American life the way it is today; it was viewed quite differently. A generation or two ago, almost no one carried any debt except for a home mortgage and maybe a car loan. There were no giant credit card balances, no payday loans (watch out for these as they tend to charge 10 percent or more for the right to your own money), and no home equity loans. In fact, just 35 years ago, the total amount of debt outstanding among all American households was about 1/600th of what it is today. That means that for every dollar your generation owes today, your grandparents' generation owed less than half a penny!

Massive debt and borrowing used to be considered un-American.
So how did so many people wind up in the hole? Over the past generation, Americans were struck by a one-two punch. The first punch
came when interest laws were changed in the late 1970s. The laws
that once limited how much interest a company could charge were
eliminated. Congress and the Supreme Court quietly took the reins
off the credit industry in the late 1970s, freeing the way for credit
card companies to jack up their interest rates and fees. And that is
exactly what they did.

To make matters worse, the credit card companies learned
something new: They could make higher profits by lending to ordinary, middle-class people than they ever made from the high-end
upper class crowd. No longer would credit cards be the exclusive
domain of the well-to-do. Instead, credit card companies would
fight to get into the wallets of every man, woman, and child in
America. Legend has it that in the United States, even the family
dog can be offered credit cards through the mail.

Why are credit card companies so eager to extend credit to
everyone? Because it turns out that if you don't pay off your balance every month, the bank can make an enormous profit. In
fact, credit card debt has become the single most profitable line
of business for big banks. Banks have found that they can get away
with slamming enormous over-the-limit fees, late fees, and interest rates on anyone who gets into trouble. The best clients for
the bank are the ones that always have a balance and never pay
it off. It is ironic that the bank's best and most profitable customers are the ones who are sliding into financial trouble—these
same people are then "rewarded" with excellent credit and higher
credit limits.

As for the second half of the one-two punch, at the same time
that credit card companies started jacking up their rates and sending offers to anyone with a pulse, more Americans found themselves struggling just to make ends meet. Job layoffs mounted, more
people lost their health insurance, medical bills skyrocketed, and
the divorce rate pushed upward. As a result, more and more people
found themselves looking for a "temporary" fix to their financial
problems. Lo and behold, there it was, that credit card offer, sitting
on the table in a stack of bills, like a life raft to a drowning man. The
temporary fix is just that—and you should always remember there
is no free lunch.

THE TRUTH ABOUT DEBT

The credit card industry is huge, and the messages it beams out are relentless:

Debt is good.
Debt is sophisticated. It makes you important.
Debt is cool.
Debt can turn you into a good friend. Debt is *your* friend.
The Truth? This is all hot air, and you know it.

Credit Card Debt Can Be Dangerous

Debt is a legal obligation to make payments each and every month—no matter what. Keep in mind that debt is handled via a contract. No matter what the future holds, debt demands to be satisfied. It is a big, hairy monster that sits in your life 24 hours a day, chanting "feed-me-feed-me-feed-me!" When times are good and you have plenty of food to feed the monster, this may not seem like a problem. You work hard; you earn a decent living, so you figure you can make the payments, no big deal, right?

Then tough times come. That's when you realize just how hungry that monster is. Maybe your hours get cut, maybe the transmission falls out, maybe you get lost for months on an interstate highway exchange. Your monster does not care. It's still hungry and at 10 percent or more in interest, it can eat you out of house and home quickly.

If you've been struggling with your debts for a long time, then you know what I'm talking about. But if you're new to the debt game, you may be thinking, "I don't remember this in the commercial." Advertisements abound, and they feature smiling couples, giggling babies, and people having "priceless" moments; in the world of debt advertisements, nothing ever goes wrong. On television, you'll never see a credit card statement with the 18 percent interest rate circled in red but for many Americans, this is credit card reality. Simple math sometimes escapes us. Think about it: If you buy something on sale at 10 percent off on a credit card with an interest rate of 18 percent, you're paying more for that item than it originally cost! Not to mention that buying anything on credit and not paying the balance immediately means paying more for the item than if you had paid cash.

Let me give you another example of dangerous debt. Banks will often charge you for getting your own money—crazy, but true. If you use an ATM machine to get $20 and you agree to the $1.50 service charge, then you are paying 7.5 percent on that transaction. That is a pretty high tax just for getting your own money. Remember that banks typically charge north of 10 percent to borrow their money via your credit card. Don't be lazy—go to the bank while they are open and use the money that you already have.

Very quickly, credit card companies found that if they wanted to rake in the profits, they just needed to keep on selling. But take a moment to really think about what they sell: very expensive money. A generation ago, it was viewed as perfectly normal not to spend money you didn't have—the line of thinking was, what if something goes wrong? But that is no longer the case.

The truth is, the debt peddlers don't want you to think about what happens when something goes wrong. Our high schools should teach classes on credit card debt and then make students take a test before getting a credit card. (Don't even get me started about how I feel about issuing credit cards to college students who typically don't work, and thus cannot repay debt, yet have little to no self-control when it comes to spending other people's money!) Debt peddlers don't want you to have that moment of doubt, that moment of clarity when you decide *not* to spend "just a little more." The less educated you are about the cost of money, the better they like it. Their only goal is to sneak that monster into your living room in the quiet hope that something will go wrong in your life.

That's right: Your credit card company wants something to go wrong. Why? Because that's when they make the most money! That's when the interest piles up, the late fees and over-the-limit charges balloon, and the bank racks up big profits from your troubles. If something goes wrong, that monster can eat everything you have. The only people that I have ever seen go bankrupt are people that do it via credit card debt or real estate debt. The credit card companies don't want you to know it, but their brand of debt is dangerous stuff.

Drowning in Debt

I realize that the previous sections might mean little to you if you are already drowning in debt. You may be thinking: I already know

how much is too much! I'm already there! What can I do to get out
from underneath this heavy burden?

Debt Ratios. First, in order to determine how much is too much,
you must calculate your debt ratio. A general guideline is 28 per-
cent/36 percent debt-to-income ratio. The 28 percent is calculated
by dividing your total monthly housing expense (mortgage, taxes,
insurance) by your total monthly pretax income. It should not
exceed 28 percent. Your total monthly pretax income should not
exceed 36 percent.

Before you borrow in excess of these amounts, seriously ask
yourself if it is both wise and necessary. After careful consideration,
you may prefer to buy a house that is smaller and more affordable
and use the extra money to furnish it. Then at least if things go
badly, you will still have a house to live in—it may be unfurnished,
but at least there will be a roof over your head.

YOU KNOW YOU'RE DROWNING IN DEBT WHEN:

- You only pay the minimum balance due every month.
- Occasionally you miss or are late with payments.
- You receive late fees, over-the-limit fees, and finance charges
  on your accounts.
- You use the grace period on a regular basis.
- You use a credit advance on one card to make the minimum
  payments on others.
- You are denied credit.
- You can't sleep due to worry about your debt.

Options When You Are Drowning in Debt

If you are hopelessly drowning in debt, bankruptcy may be one
option. Be advised that while bankruptcy forgives many debts,
some—like child support, federal income taxes, and some student
loans—are not erased.

Chapter 7 bankruptcy allows you to keep certain minimal
exempt assets as determined by the state in which you live and it
eliminates many debts. Nonexempt assets are liquidated, and creditors share the proceeds.

In Chapter 13 bankruptcy, creditors agree to take a lower amount than the balance due and your assets are not liquidated as long as you make the required payments. This option is generally available only if you have a steady income.

Either form of bankruptcy remains on your credit report for up to ten years, and it may affect your ability to obtain rental housing as well as future credit. Remember that bankruptcy laws are always changing and it is up to you to stay educated regarding your rights. This may sound controversial, but sometimes it would be better for you to enter bankruptcy and wipe out debt if you are not ever going to ever pay it off. It is important that you save money for retirement and struggling for ten or more years to pay down your debt while not saving for retirement certainly won't get you where you need to be.

Credit Negotiation. Many creditors will negotiate directly with you for a lower total payment or reduced interest rates to help you avoid filing for bankruptcy. To the extent that actual debt is forgiven, the debt forgiveness is considered to be taxable income. I know this for a fact because I went through it. I came out of college with $6,000 in credit card debt. All I have to show for it is a Bobby Brown CD (which I still own and never listen to). It stands as a reminder of why I avoid debt. At first, I tried to service the debt (sort of). For a while I did ok. Then out of nowhere I started missing payments and the next thing I knew it was $10,000 of debt. Months passed and I actually told the collection agencies that I had died. I called my creditors and said I was either going bankrupt or they could settle for 60 cents on the dollar. They took my offer.

Debt Consolidation. Certain organizations, such as Consumer Credit Counseling Services (www.ccsintl.org), will contact creditors on your behalf to negotiate for lower balances and generally lower interest rates. You pay a nominal fee to use their services. Credit consolidation may be considered a negative on your credit report and reduce your overall credit score. I suggest consumer credit counseling as the intermediate step between the time you get into problems and going bankrupt.

Debt Repayment. Repaying debt impacts your credit score positively. While this method isn't easy, people who choose this path feel a tremendous sense of accomplishment and satisfaction when they are finally debt free. To accomplish debt repayment, you need to create a budget and stick to it. It will take time, but if you do the math correctly then you will eventually be able to get out of debt. Don't forget to tell the credit card companies your situation and that you have a plan. Sometimes they will waive past penalties as a way of rewarding you: Remember, they want to keep you as a debt servicing customer, not a tax write-off for money lost.

Target Debt. Over the long term, you will be better off financially if you pay off the debt with the highest interest rate first. However, for some immediate gratification, you may wish to knock out the debts with the lower balances as soon as you can. There are no rules about which is the right way or wrong way to fix your problem. The math does dictate that you tackle the higher interest rate debts first, but if you need motivation to keep you on budget, then go after the smaller debt right away.

Paying off bad debt is critical to your financial freedom. It is as difficult as it is rewarding, and once you're finished, you will find yourself on a new path of strength, ready to accumulate your wealth. So get organized and start today!

HOME SWEET HOME 4

QUESTION: Is it better to buy or rent a place to live?

ANSWER: Your choice depends on several factors. While financial factors can be carefully weighed and measured, the intangibles of owning property may appeal to you the most. Today, as in the past, home ownership remains the quintessential American dream. However, a big factor in your decision might be that it is cheaper to rent than to buy. In this case, perhaps it makes the most financial sense for you to rent for a few years and and make the maximum contribution to your retirement plan possible. After building a nice nest egg, then you may consider buying your own home.

TAX BREAKS FOR HOMES

Home ownership offers a number of tax breaks. On your Schedule A, under the Itemized Deductions section, you can deduct mortgage interest (on your principal residence and a second home), property taxes, points paid on a new loan, and points paid on a refinanced loan (must be amortized over the life of the loan). When selling your home at a profit, gains of up to $250,000 per person ($500,000 for married couples filing jointly) are tax free if you have lived in your principal residence during at least two of the last five years. Better yet, you can use this same exemption after living in another home for at least two years of the last five.

RETURN ON INVESTMENT

A return on investment (ROI) is a measure of profitability. ROI measures how effectively you use capital to generate profit; the higher the ROI, the better.

Is the return on the investment an incentive to own versus rent? Let's do the math:

A typical down payment is 20 percent of the home's value. For a $150,000 purchase, that's $30,000. If that same home's value increases 2 percent next year to $153,000, the return (ignoring taxes) is more than 2 percent because of the leverage from the down payment. Divide that $3,000 (increase in value) by $30,000 (the down payment), and it leaves you with a 10 percent return.

BREAK-EVEN HOME PURCHASES

As a general guideline, to cover the costs of buying or selling a property (mortgage, appraisal, application, inspection, moving, title insurance, legal costs, real estate commissions) plus the regular costs of home ownership, a property has to appreciate in value at least 15 percent. This generally takes five years, depending on location and markets.

Of course, you need to consider other factors when calculating your total return, such as closing costs, mortgage interest, equity build-up in the home, repairs and maintenance while owning the home, utilities, wear and tear, and tax savings. Leverage can work to your advantage with a home purchase as long as the home appreciates. Leverage can work against you when home values drop.

Remember that Donald Trump (considered by most to be a very successful real estate investor) has been bankrupt several times because he was overleveraged and could no longer service his debt.

QUALIFYING FOR A MORTGAGE

A mortgage is a loan for the specific purpose of financing the purchase of real estate, usually with specified payment periods and interest rates. The borrower (mortgagee) gives the lender (mortgagor) a lien on the property as collateral for the loan.

Unlike the credit card debt (bad debt) discussed in Chapter 3, mortgage debt is generally considered to be good debt. Nevertheless, most potential borrowers are nervous about getting a mortgage loan because they share a widespread misconception: They believe they have no bargaining power relative to lenders. That *was* the way things worked for much of our history (and the way things still are in much of the world), but it has not been true in the United States for many years. Today lenders compete fiercely to make good loans to creditworthy customers. The Internet has not lowered the cost of mortgages but it has given the consumer a lot of information and a ton of options.

A "good loan" is one made to a borrower who has both the *ability* and the *willingness* to repay it.

If you can demonstrate both the ability and the willingness to repay, lenders will be anxious for your business. *You* are in the driver's seat and thus you can negotiate and ask for better terms. Be a savvy consumer. Learn to ask for the best loan terms possible as this is a huge financial commitment. Always keep in mind that if you don't ask, you won't receive.

If your position is weak on the ability/willingness score, you will be limited to lenders who specialize in weak applicants and are prepared to take larger risks. These lenders are fewer in number, and their interest rates and other terms will be less favorable than those available to stronger applicants. Remember, the mortgage market is all about the math. Lenders know that a certain percentage of borrowers will fail to pay them back. Accordingly, they spread their risk among low interest loans for great credit and higher interest loans for poor credit. They will make their money either way—from the consistent payments of quality customers or from the higher rates and fees assessed to less qualified borrowers.

Determining the borrower's *ability* to repay is what qualification is all about. Determining the borrower's *willingness* to repay is determined largely by an applicant's past credit history. For a loan to be approved, the lender must be satisfied on both scores. This is the difference between qualification and approval.

The process of making a final determination on approval or rejection is called underwriting. Underwriting involves verifying the information that has been obtained from the borrower and that served as the basis for qualification, as well as assessing information on the applicant's creditworthiness.

Qualification and Affordability

Qualification is always relative to property value. That is, a borrower who is well qualified to purchase a $300,000 house may not qualify to buy a $400,000 house.

The property value for which you can qualify depends on your personal financial condition, as well as on the mortgage terms available in the market at the time you are shopping. Example: To afford a $400,000 house, you need about $54,400 in cash, which assumes a 10 percent down payment. With a 7 percent interest rate on your mortgage, your monthly income should be at least $11,200 and (if this is your income) your monthly payments on existing debt should not exceed $895.00.[1]

---

[1] These numbers are estimates, mainly because of variations in closing costs and in taxes and insurance.

Meeting Income Requirements

Lenders ask two basic questions about the borrower's ability to pay. First, is the borrower's income large enough to service the new expenses associated with the loan, plus any existing debt obligations that will continue in the future? Second, does the borrower have enough cash to meet the up-front cash requirements of the transaction? The lender must be satisfied on both counts. The truth is that qualifying to borrow money has gotten easier over the past 20 years. Lenders have relaxed their standards in order to keep business flowing and to generate higher revenues.

Expense Ratios

In general, the lender assesses the adequacy of the borrower's income based on two ratios that have become standard:

- The first is known as the housing expense ratio. This is the sum of the monthly mortgage payment including mortgage insurance, property taxes, and hazard insurance divided by the borrower's monthly income.
- The second is the total expense ratio. This is the same except that the numerator includes the borrower's existing debt service obligations. For each of their loan programs, lenders set maximums for these ratios, such as 28 percent and 36 percent, which the actual ratios must not exceed.

Private Mortgage Insurance

QUESTION: I want to buy a home but don't have a 20 percent down payment. I have heard that I can get around this using PMI. What is PMI?

ANSWER: Private mortgage insurance (PMI) allows people to purchase a home with a smaller-than-usual down payment. In return for the smaller down payment, the borrower pays a premium (included in the monthly mortgage). So, although your down payment is lower, your monthly payments may be higher ($20 to $100 more per month on a $100,000 loan) because of the added cost of the insurance. In essence, you are paying for the lender to carry an insurance policy on your mortgage loan in the event of your default. While mortgage interest is tax deductible, PMI is not.

Avoid PMI

Private Mortgage Insurance (PMI) is mortgage insurance provided by nongovernment insurers that protects a lender against loss if the borrower defaults. Basically, it allows the lenders to cover themselves in the event that you don't pay them back.

PMI is considered a necessary evil for some borrowers but avoid PMI if you can. Often, in order to eliminate the need for PMI, you must settle for a mortgage with a higher interest rate. The lender purchases the mortgage insurance, and you pay the additional cost through higher interest rates over the life of your loan.

The way you finance your home also can make a difference; 80/10/10, for example, means that you apply for two mortgages. Your primary mortgage is for 80 percent of the home's value, the second mortgage is for 10 percent, and you make a 10 percent down payment.

Calculating the cost benefit of paying PMI versus structuring your financing to avoid PMI must be done on a case-by-case basis, so that when all is said and done, you avoid overpaying.

OTHER FACTORS TO CONSIDER WHEN BUYING A HOME

Let's say you sell your primary residence and move to your vacation home on the beach, pocketing a large, tax-free gain. Home prices skyrocket, and it's too crowded at the beach, so you sell the beach house and get another large chunk of cash tax-free. Then you move to Des Moines, Iowa, which has one of the lowest average costs of housing in America, and live happily ever after.

Unless you live in an area that has escalating home prices, you may never see a sharp spike in your home's market value. But that's OK. Slow, steady growth is good, too. Don't buy a home and expect it to go up in value every single year. Real estate tends to move higher when jobs are created and wages go higher and this tends to happen in bursts, not in a steady stream.

Wherever you live, the essential rule in home buying is location. If you're buying a first home, start small with the lowest-priced home in the best neighborhood, then work to fix up and maintain your home so it keeps pace with other properties in your neighborhood. Check out the school districts. Good schools make a difference when you sell. Check to see if there are quality hospitals and colleges nearby. Colleges tend to create jobs, which help create value in your property because people want to live near their work.

If you're thinking about a condominium or townhouse, check the quality of the construction carefully, especially the soundproofing. Talk to other condo residents; verify that most of the units are owner occupied and review the financial status of the complex to make sure the homeowners' association is doing its job to maintain the property and control expenses. Remember, homeowner fees are never ever totally paid off so your investment will never be free and clear.

RENTING VERSUS BUYING A HOME

Buying your first home is one of the most exciting milestones in life. It also is a pretty intense as well as anxious time in your life. Trading in your rent for a mortgage payment can be a wise investment, but for some, renting may be advantageous. Renting means you pay no maintenance, property taxes, or repair costs if something breaks. Estimates are that for every dollar a homeowner spends to buy a home, they spend $1.50 on interest, repairs, maintenance, property taxes, and other costs.

Renters can save or invest the money that a homeowner typically would spend on a new roof, property taxes, or landscaping. I believe that maxing out your 401(k) or retirement plan is more important than buying a home only because your ability to work and earn income runs out when you retire. By then, you had better have saved enough to last through your golden years, otherwise retirement might not be all it is cracked up to be. Renters also often have access to amenities like pools and exercise facilities and depending upon the complex in which they live, enjoy a sense of community. Nice homes may also be available for rent in good neighborhoods at reasonable prices. If you relocate to a new city, consider renting first as a way to learn about the community before buying.

However, if renting no longer makes sense for you and you are thinking about breaking things off with your landlord, you need to be properly informed before you make your move. Take your time and write down some of your thoughts. Here are a few things you may want to consider.

Advantages of Renting
- More of your costs are fixed so you know what to expect.
- Flexibility: You can leave when your lease is up.
- There is no risk of losing equity in your investment.
- There is less maintenance.
- You incur lower up-front costs.

Advantages of Buying
- Even if your property value stays stagnant, over time your equity will build and your balance due will decrease.
- Flexibility in remodeling: Go ahead and paint your bedroom purple—it's yours.
- Tax advantages: You can deduct the interest you pay from your income tax.

Disadvantages of Renting
- You have no equity to gain.
- You have little or no say in the home's upkeep.
- You receive no tax advantages.

Disadvantages of Buying
- Costs are variable.
- The equity you receive will be unpredictable.
- In most cases, if you want to move you must first sell your home.
- You have responsibility for repairs and repair costs—you're the super when the toilet breaks.
- Up-front costs are generally higher.

WHAT'S THE RIGHT MORTGAGE?

QUESTION: I am trying to figure out how much mortgage I can afford. Neighbors tell me one thing, financial planners tell me another, while my mortgage broker tells me that I can afford more than what both of them told me. Why the difference?

ANSWER: Never take financial advice from a neighbor (or a friend, family member, the guy who cuts your hair, etc.). Mortgage lenders and financial planners often have different ideas on how much mortgage a person can afford. The planner will often suggest a lower amount as he or she is looking at the bigger picture (i.e., your retirement and college savings).

Buyer Beware

Mortgage lenders are in business to lend money and have lots of experience assessing credit risks. Guidelines—mortgage debt should be less than 28 percent of gross income, total debt less than 36 percent—are based on lending as much money as possible while maintaining an acceptable default rate. If you are above 36 percent then you are putting your financial future at risk. That is okay as long as you understand the risk. The guidelines provide for a basic standard of living in addition to the mortgage, but do not, on a case-by-case basis, account for individual needs and circumstances. A financial planner looks at your total financial picture—not just the housing facet. From sending the kids to college to vacation preferences and retirement issues, the financial planner knows all and sees all—and plans accordingly. Mortgage companies also focus on the mortgage time frame, not your lifetime or long-term goals such as building a retirement nest egg. Your financial planner, on the other hand, does factor such goals into a recommended mortgage amount. From a financial planning perspective, it's important to factor lifetime goals into the mortgage company's affordability calculations.

Choosing the Best Loan

QUESTION: I am about to purchase/refinance a home. What type of loan should I choose?

ANSWER: Consumers today have plenty of options. There really seems to be a mortgage for every type of consumer. Among them are fixed-rate mortgages for terms of 15, 20, or 30 years; adjustable-rate mortgages (ARMs) and balloon mortgages; FHA/VA loans; and niche programs such as first-time home buyer, 100 percent programs, and loans for the credit challenged.

LOAN TERMS DEFINED

Fixed-Rate Mortgage. Fixed-rate mortgages are the most popular form of mortgage, one that allows you to lock in an interest rate for the term of your loan. These mortgages are also called conventional loans. With fixed-rate mortgages, the rate, payment, and term remain constant from the day you sign the mortgage agreement, regardless of market fluctuations and inflation. The payment is less with a 30-year mortgage than with the 15-year variety, but the trade-off is that you pay more interest.

For example:
On a 5.5 percent fixed-rate $150,000 mortgage of 15 years, the monthly payment is $1,226 and the total interest paid is $70,613.

A 30-year loan on the same amount of money carries an $852.00 monthly payment and $156,606 in interest.

Choose a fixed-rate if you plan to stay in your home for more than seven years or if you like knowing that the monthly payment will not change.

Adjustable-Rate Mortgage (ARM). An adjustable rate mortgage is the second most popular type of mortgage. An ARM has a fixed rate and payment for the initial specified time (less than 30 years); then it can change every year after that. With a 3/1 ARM for example, the payment and rate is fixed for the first three years, then can fluctuate annually based on an index like the one-year Treasury Securities Index, London Interbank Offered Rates (LIBOR), or Cost of Funds Index (COFI). Lenders also add a margin, most commonly 2.75 percent, to determine the new rate. ARMs have caps on how high a rate can change per adjustment (called a ceiling)—most often 2 percent over the starting rate. ARMs usually start with better rates than fixed rate mortgages in order to compensate the borrower for the additional risk that future interest rate fluctuations will create.

Balloon Mortgage. Balloon mortgages are more risky. The payment and rate are fixed for the initial term, after which the loan principal balance is due. A balloon loan will often have the advantage of very low interest payments, thus requiring very little capital outlay during the life of the loan. Because most of the repayment is deferred until the end of the payment period, the borrower has substantial flexibility to utilize the available capital during the life of the loan. The major problem with such a loan is that the borrower needs to be self-disciplined in preparing for the large single payment, since interim payments are not being made. Balloon loans are often undertaken when refinancing or when a major cash flow event is anticipated. At this point, you decide whether pay off the loan or refinance at current market rates. Unlike the ARM, there is no cap with a balloon mortgage.

ARMs or balloons make sense if you relocate frequently or plan to stay in the house a short time. Choose an ARM carefully if this is your first home. The lower initial rates mean that you can qualify for a more expensive home, but remember, the payment can rise, and you need to be prepared. Many lenders qualify you for your ARM loan based upon the initial rate plus the first cap.

FHA Loans. The Federal Housing Administration (FHA), is a government agency whose primary purpose is to insure residential mortgage loans. It is an agency within the Department of Housing and Urban Development (HUD) and was established in 1934 to increase home ownership in America among the middle class. It accomplishes this mission by facilitating less stringent loan qualifications, such as 3 percent down payment, higher qualifying ratios (29/41,whereas conventional loans are 28/36), more flexible qualifying guidelines, limitations on buyers' closing costs, and allowing closing costs to satisfy part of the down payment requirement. For more information, visit their Web site at http://www.hud.gov/offices/hsg/fhahistory.cfm.

VA Loans. The Veteran's Administrations (VA) also guarantees loans to eligible veterans that are made by private lenders such as banks and mortgage companies. To determine if you are eligible for a VA loan, you should request a certificate of eligibility from the VA. VA loan features include no down payment, no monthly mortgage insurance premiums, and limits on closing costs. For more information, visit their Web site at www.homeloans.va.gov.

Niche Programs. Buying your first home is an exciting enterprise. Many lenders have special programs for first-time homebuyers. These programs offer special interest rates, give credits toward closing costs, expand your purchasing power by allowing higher qualifying ratios (33/38), and even have 97 or 100 percent financing. Check local, state, and federal housing programs to see if you qualify for any special programs.

First-time homebuyers should *always* ask lenders if they offer special programs or cash incentives. The more questions you ask, the more informed you will be. The more information that you have, the less stressed you will be about making your decisions.

Loans for Credit-Challenged. If you have had credit problems, don't despair (but do try to fix your credit). Certain lenders have mortgage financing for you. There is a catch though. You'll pay higher interest rates, but often, if you try to improve your credit score, you can refinance later at a better rate. Use this financing as a tool to help you get back on track.

DETERMINING WHEN TO REFINANCE

QUESTION: When interest rates are low, there is a lot of talk about refinancing. How can I determine the right time to refinance my mortgage?

ANSWER: There are many reasons to consider refinancing your mortgage, including a lower interest rate, a lower monthly payment, a shorter loan term, and extra cash for home improvements or debt consolidation.

When Refinancing Makes Sense

Before you refinance ask yourself three questions:

1. How long do you plan to stay in the home?
2. How much can you reduce your interest rate?
3. How much will it cost to get the new loan?

Though you often hear that it makes sense to refinance your mortgage if you can reduce your rate by at least 2 percent, that guideline is too high, in most cases. Often, a person can benefit from lower interest rate differentials depending on how long they plan to remain in the home. It's important to analyze your break-even point. I suggest meeting with a mortgage lender versus a bank. This is because mortgage lenders want your business but can put you into many different products in order to get it. Banks, on the other hand, tend to push a product that may or may not be right for you.

Points or No Points?

The same analysis can be applied to the question of whether you would be wise to pay points in order to obtain a lower rate. The best calculators take into account several factors, including your refinancing costs, tax bracket, how rapidly the principal is paid down, the time-value of money, and the rate your money could earn if you did not use it to refinance. Don't assume that paying points is bad. A lot of lenders advertise "no points" as a selling feature in order to get your business even though they don't know your unique situation. Their marketing strategy makes little sense. You have to run the numbers in order to know what will work best for you.

Changing from a 30-Year to a 15-Year Loan

Reducing the term of your loan is an easy way to reduce your rate and save thousands of dollars in interest. As noted previously, you must analyze the break-even period. Reducing the term can be accomplished without a significant increase in the monthly payment when the rate difference is large enough.

If the monthly payment will significantly increase, be careful not to overextend yourself. Being "house poor" is no fun. Is your

employment secure? Can you handle the larger payments if unem-
ployment strikes? Also, keep in mind that making regular extra
principal payments on a 30-year loan offers you flexibility and can
save you thousands of dollars of interest in the long run. On the
other hand, prepaying your mortgage while not funding your
401(k) or retirement plan can be a sure way to end up house rich
and cash poor in retirement.

Swapping an ARM for a Fixed-Rate

This is a tough decision that requires rate speculation. You'll want
to consider how long you plan to stay in the home, the cost of a new
loan, and how today's interest rates compare to historical rates. If
you think short-term rates are going to rise then it might make
sense to lock in a long-term fixed rate. Ultimately, only you can
decide what's comfortable for you.

Cashing Out on Refinancing to Consolidate Debt

Consolidating debt (e.g., credit care balances) at a lower, tax-
deductible interest rate usually makes a lot of sense on paper. In
real life, though, it can turn a short-term problem into a long-term
debt. Also, this serial borrowing strategy often repeats itself, with
the homeowner habitually racking up debt, pulling out the equity
in the home and jeopardizing a debt-free retirement. Make sure
you can be honest with yourself. Revisit the strategies in Chapters 1
and 2: Talk to your spouse and write down your plans on paper.
(Your spouse should do the same.) Exchange the pieces of paper,
as it makes both of you more accountable. Thoroughly discuss
your "best-case scenario" intentions and force yourselves to examine what would happen if things don't go as well as you have them
set out on paper.

If you must consolidate, make sure that you have addressed the
issues that made it necessary to consolidate your debts in the first
place. Correcting bad spending habits helps to insure that history
doesn't repeat itself. Remember: You are putting your home up as
collateral. If consolidation is your goal, it may be more cost effective for you to use a home equity loan or credit line due to lower
loan acquisition costs. If you choose an equity line of credit, avoid
making interest-only payments. It works the same as it does with

credit cards: If you only pay the minimum, the balance will never go away. Be honest with yourself and each other about your ability to repay the loan—remember, this is your future!

FINDING THE BEST LOAN

Once you decide that refinancing is cost effective, consider using a mortgage broker to find the best loan. A good broker can shop many lenders effectively and is especially helpful if your credit is less than perfect. Be diligent in comparing costs and, when you decide to lock in the rate, be sure to get it in writing. Insist that your mortgage broker disclose all sources of compensation, including broker's markup (how much higher your rate is than the wholesale rate). Ask your broker to take you to lunch and get to know one another. (They will make a pretty penny on you, so don't be afraid to ask them for something simple like lunch.) Ask a lot of questions because as we already know, knowledge is power. You might look for a broker who will work for a flat fee.

HELPFUL WEB SITES FOR
RESEARCHING LOANS

- http://www.mtgprofessor.com
- http://www.mortgage-x.com
- http://www.hsh.com
- http://www.bankrate.com

REFINANCING A MORTGAGE
AND TAKING A LINE OF CREDIT

QUESTION: Interest rates have dropped since I purchased a home, and I need money to make improvements to the house. Should I refinance my mortgage?

ANSWER: Whether or not to refinance depends upon several factors, including the change in interest rates, the remaining term of your mortgage, and the cost of the refinancing. There are also some cash flow and income tax considerations. My personal opinion is that you should not finance home improvements via a refi-

nance on your home. I tend to favor strategy and disciplined saving
as investment cogs. When you refinance it seems like you are getting "easy money" and there is a tendency to want to improve the
home. Bear in mind that home improvements generally only return
60 cents on the dollar so they are not wise investments. However,
they do make you happy and that is certainly worth something; consider saving up for them.

The Basics—Interest Rates, Points, and Mortgage Term

A good rule of thumb for refinancing is: You should refinance only
if the new rate is *at least* 1 percent less than your existing rate. This
ensures that the refinance is advantageous enough to cover the
transaction costs involved. Points or prepaid interest charges for a
new mortgage are also a critical factor. One point equals 1 percent
of the total amount borrowed. You can buy down your interest rate
by paying additional points or buy down the points by paying a
higher interest rate. In a refinance transaction, you generally want
to avoid paying points for several reasons, including the tax treatment of points in a refinance. You really need to sit down and run
numbers (and yes, I know that sounds cliché but it is true). Sometimes you will get smaller payments now but risk the potential for
higher future payments and sometimes you will get a higher payment now but with little risk of change in the future. You must
decide what works for you.

You also need to consider the term or life of the existing loan
versus that of the new loan. You may decide to refinance because of
lower rates, your present loan has a balloon provision, you currently
have an ARM, or to extend the loan term.

Home Remodeling Considerations

If you're thinking about making home improvements, a home equity
line of credit (HEL) or refinancing your mortgage for a higher
amount can be helpful. Remember though that a HEL is a second
mortgage and if you fail to repay it then you will lose your home. Consider worst-case scenarios before tapping into that type of loan.

A home equity line of credit allows you to draw money from the
bank on an as-needed basis, up to the maximum amount of the

credit line. Interest rates generally are tied to and fluctuate with the Prime Rate, so the monthly payment changes.

> The Prime Rate is the interest rate that commercial banks charge their most creditworthy borrowers, such as large corporations. The prime rate is also called prime.

Home equity loans are for a fixed term and interest rate. The entire amount of the loan is drawn when the loan is established. Lines and loans generally require less paperwork and involve fewer loan fees and closing costs than traditional mortgages. Home equity interest is tax deductible as long as the loan does not exceed $100,000.

If you decide to refinance your mortgage, the mortgage interest is generally tax deductible. If you pay points on the refinance, the points on the amount of the loan used for the remodeling or expansion are deductible. However, the points attributable to the existing loan must be amortized and deducted over the life of the loan.

Always Think It Through

Allow yourself some financial flexibility. You don't want your mortgage and/or home equity payments to create undue hardship should your monthly income suddenly drop. Look for a loan with no prepayment penalties, and consult a qualified tax advisor to accurately evaluate the tax ramifications of changes in your home mortgage. Try to find something that you are comfortable with in both a best-case and worst-case scenario.

SAVE MONEY VIA REFINANCING

QUESTION: We recently refinanced our home and have improved our cash flow by $200 a month. What should we do with the funds created as a result of our reduced mortgage payment?

ANSWER: Depending on your current mortgage rate, refinancing at today's lower rates can indeed result in reduced monthly payments.

There are several good options on what to do with your additional cash flow. The following are some options.

Good Uses for Savings from Refinancing
- Increase your retirement savings.
- Pay down credit cards and consumer loans.
- Open a Roth IRA.
- Create or add to your emergency fund.
- Shore up your insurance coverage.

This new monthly surplus is an excellent opportunity to grow your wealth. Don't blow it on something you don't need now for something you *will* need later—retirement! Remember: The extra cash flow you enjoy now while you are working is a luxury that you won't have when you retire.

USING YOUR HOME EQUITY WISELY

QUESTION: Some of my neighbors seem to be remodeling their homes, taking grand vacations, and buying fancy cars. I've been told they are using home equity loans to finance these things. Are they squandering their hard-earned equity?

ANSWER: Home equity loans are ultimately a second mortgage so use the money wisely because you are putting yourself in the position to lose your home.

Smart Choices for Utilizing Home Equity Lines of Credit
- Debt consolidation. The interest is tax deductible.
- Investments that increase in value. Make sure that an addition or renovation will increase your home's value.
- Education funding. Determine the estimated cost of your children's education. Depending on when your children will enter college, determine how much must be set aside, and at what rate of return, in order to meet funding needs.
- A source of emergency money. A home equity line of credit, also known as a HELOC, is good to have in place in the event of an emergency or to seize an opportunity. A HELOC is simply a line of credit secured by a second mortgage on your home,

and it is accessed via a checkbook and/or debit card. The size of the HELOC is limited by the amount of equity you have in your home. Please take careful note of the word "emergency." A new car is not an emergency nor is a new flat screen TV considered an emergency in any book.

MORTGAGE ACCELERATION

QUESTION: I think I would like to pay off my mortgage early. Should I spend my extra money this way?

ANSWER: This is a long-standing debate. The answer involves your personal circumstances and feelings about debt. The answer also involves an idea called "opportunity costs." When you prepay money into a mortgage you lose the ability to put that money elsewhere and perhaps earn a better rate of return than the amount that you are saving via prepaying and lowering your mortgage obligation. Crunching your particular numbers is the best method for determining whether or not prepayment makes sense for you. Remember that the primary benefits to prepaying a mortgage are realizing substantial savings on interest and the peace of mind that comes with paying off a debt. Prepayment has no effect on the sales value of your home, although it obviously does affect how much money you will get out of the house when you sell it.

Prepaying Your Mortgage: Money Down the Drain?

I know the idea of not prepaying your mortgage will be offensive to some. Just bear with me and read through this section anyway.

In an ideal world, people want to pay off their mortgage because debt is a dirty word. After all, the word mortgage has its roots in *mort*, the French word for death, which certainly echoes the dread of being in debt. A mortgage is often viewed as one of life's darker burdens. Our parents taught us to look forward to the day we pay off the debt and own our home free and clear. In the past, Americans used to celebrate their last house payment with a mortgage burning party.

There is no question that debt is the flip side of making money. You can't separate the two. There is good debt (low-interest and tax benefit mortgage) and there is bad debt (high-interest credit card, automobile, or personal loan debt). Managed well, debt can put you in a stronger financial position. If we all had to pay cold, hard cash for everything, most of us might never own a house or perhaps even a car. But the key is to be the master of your debt. It is important to gain control over debt and not let debt control you.

My own mother is in her 70s and she has a 30-year mortgage. My father passed away over ten years ago and my mother has never worked outside the home. Again, I repeat, she has a 30-year mortgage and will likely never pay it off. Today, you just don't need to pay off your home. In fact, for most it's a foolish idea. Why?

Inexperienced money handlers want to pay off the house because they see it as a large burden. No doubt that it is, but it is a burden that you signed up for. Paying it off makes little sense as houses usually appreciate at the rate of inflation (give or take) so whether you prepay or not, it will either go up in value or it won't. You can prepay in various ways: by adding a little extra to your regular monthly payment; by making one extra payment a year; or by paying biweekly rather than monthly (making half a monthly payment every two weeks), which comes out to one extra full payment each year. For most people, these various forms of prepayment are a big mistake. Many couples fight about this, especially those whose parents had differing views about the opportunity cost of money.

The idea seems right, doesn't it? Prepaying can pare years off your mortgage and reduce your total interest. Interest payments seem obnoxious when you look at how much you pay in interest over the years. Prepaying on a 7 percent loan seems to strike people as though they are making 7 percent (or at least not losing 7 percent) on their money. For example, by paying $25 extra each month on a fixed-rate, 30-year, $100,000 mortgage, at 7 percent interest, you'd save $18,214 in total interest and shorten the term by more than three years.

Before you get carried away thinking about saving thousands of dollars, look deeper to determine if prepaying is a wise move for you. Prepaying is far more of an emotional decision than a financial one. Emotions aside, you need to consider several factors before deciding to prepay. It is never a good idea to prepay a mortgage if you have consumer debt such as credit card debt. Individuals can free up and do more with their money by paying off higher rate credit cards than by prepaying their mortgages. Why pay off your cheap mortgage debt when you really ought to be paying off that pricey credit card?

Also, be sure prepaying won't cramp your ability to save for other financial goals. Sometimes people end up house poor.

> Being house poor means that you have the house paid off, but you haven't saved for other goals, such as retirement or the children's college education. People who are house poor end up having to refinance their house or perhaps even sell it in order to get the capital they need to meet those other goals.

Is is also financially risky to have most or all of your assets tied up in one thing, your house in this case. Sometimes neighborhoods go bad, the local economy sours, or the house next door to you gets converted into a fraternity house and your house is no longer worth what you thought it would be. I know it sounds odd to consider such unusual circumstances but I assure you that I am being a friend by bringing up worst-case scenarios for you to consider. Remember, if you sock all your assets into the house and get it paid off then you will ultimately be house rich, but one piece of bad luck could leave you house poor and possibly cash poor.

Another factor to weigh is your liquidity needs. By prepaying your mortgage, you could end up strapped for cash to cover regular bills or emergency expenses. Let's say that you get a rare disease that causes a stalk of corn to grow out of your ear and you need emergency money to have surgery in Mexico (the only corn-removal expert in the world is located there). Trying to get your hands on money that is tied up in your house can be time consuming and costly. Another example of liquidity problems occurs when people lose their jobs after years of prepaying a mortgage. Unless you have another source of cash that will keep you making those mortgage payments, you are still delinquent after missing one payment. Before even considering prepaying on a mortgage, make sure you have at least two to three months of cash built up for emergency situations.

Tax consequences also must weigh into your prepayment decision. Usually, consumers think about putting extra money into the mortgage during their peak earning years, between ages 40 and 60. It is not very smart to be in the highest tax bracket of your life and to get rid of your largest tax deduction by prepaying your mortgage. Paying less in taxes means you have more income on your bottom line, which frees you up to make stronger long-term financial decisions.

For instance, if your mortgage rate is 7 percent, putting money into your mortgage is like investing it at 7 percent—or so it seems on the surface. But you can't forget the tax effects. Say you are in the 28 percent tax bracket. By giving up your tax deduction on mortgage interest, you lose 28 percent of your "earnings" on your investment. That means you only get 72 percent (100% − 28%) of that 7 percent interest rate, or 5.04 percent (.72 × 7%).

Now, compare that with what you could earn by placing your money somewhere besides your mortgage. Suppose you were to invest in a mutual fund earning 10 percent. (The long-term historical return on the market is 11 percent.) If you're in the 28 percent tax bracket, you lose 28 percent to taxes. In other words, you earn 72 percent (100%−28%) of that 10 percent interest rate, or 7.2 percent. The upshot in this particular example is that you are ahead by more than two percentage points if you put your money into the mutual fund instead of into your mortgage. You would be even further ahead if that money went into a tax-advantaged plan, such as an individual retirement account (IRA) or 401(k).

On an emotional level, it is easy to see why people are diverting investment money into their home mortgage instead of putting it into stocks or bonds. That actually might look attractive these days, with the way these vehicles are underperforming. When you prepay your remaining mortgage with a lump sum, or accelerate the payoff through monthly extra principal payments, you reduce your long-term interest costs. On a 30-year, 7.5-percent, $200,000 mortgage, paying an extra $200 a month would save $112,625 in interest charges. Thus, paying off a mortgage carrying 7 to 8 percent looks like a smart move compared with investing in stocks, which have been on the skids since March of 2000. It also looks smarter compared with 10-year Treasury bonds currently yielding a modest 4.5 percent, or even the more anemic returns of money market mutual funds, savings accounts, and certificates of deposit.

Here is the reality. Let's say you will be in the 27-percent federal income tax bracket next year. Thus, the real cost of that 7.5-percent mortgage (which is the same as the return you would get prepaying the mortgage) is 5.47 percent. Someone in the top 38.6-percent tax bracket next year is actually paying only 4.6 percent on their mortgage (this doesn't take into account any state taxes saved).

Compare this with the after-tax return of an alternative investment. A stock returning 7.5 percent annually provides an after-tax return of 6 percent assuming a 20-percent long-term capital gains tax. In dollar terms, putting $200 monthly toward stocks earning 7.5 percent annually would earn $271,174 in 30 years, versus the $112, 625 you saved in interest payments by prepaying the mortgage. The added plus here is that the money you save is liquid versus the mortgage prepayment, which is gone forever and can't be used in emergencies.

Let me take one final shot at the interest that you save by prepaying. Interest savings gained from prepaying a mortgage are overstated because of the time value of money. Due to inflation, the interest payments you make in the latter years of your mortgage are made with much cheaper dollars than the ones made with the early payments. So prepaying means you're using up dollars that are more valuable.

Another argument for continuing to invest in stocks instead of diverting the money into the mortgage is that stocks overall might be considered a bargain these days because they are so beaten down. The assumption is that stocks, while returning poorly now, will eventually recover their losses, and much more, in the long run, so it's a good time to buy them while they are cheap. Since 1926, stocks have averaged annually 7.9 percent after taxes and inflation are taken into account [Vanguard's retirement booklet]—well above the return you'd earn paying off a mortgage early. An even more near-term perspective can be seen in that the stock market has performed poorly over the three-year period from 2000 through 2002, losing an average of about 14 percent annually; its ten-year annualized pretax return is still about 9 percent as measured by the Standard & Poor's 500 Index.

I will concede that for conservative investors who don't invest in stocks, or perhaps even bonds, prepaying your mortgage might make financial sense, say many financial planners. You'll probably earn more than you would with the low-risk alternatives and you'll reduce your debt, which is usually a good thing, especially in tough times.

Despite all of the good reasons I've just mentioned, I am not saying that mortgage prepayment is never a good idea. If you are free of consumer debt, have saved amply for retirement and the kids' education, have a healthy cash reserve fund, and won't get boosted into the next tax bracket by losing your tax deduction, then prepaying may be the right move. If you are risk-averse and prefer to invest conservatively, you'll usually get ahead financially by prepaying your mortgage rather than by investing in certificates, for example.

If you do prepay then please, whenever you do pay an extra amount on your mortgage, be sure to apply it to the principal. Check first to find out if there is a prepayment penalty (such mortgage penalties are rare, especially in credit unions, but check anyway). Prepayment penalties can come in a variety of forms with the most common being that you can't prepay more than 5 percent of the value of the mortgage in any given year.

Besides making extra payments spread over time, another approach is to set up an escrow or investment account to accumulate assets, and then pay off your mortgage in one lump sum at retirement, when you'd prefer to have no mortgage payments hanging over your head. Presumably your tax bracket will be lower at this phase of your life, and you won't need the tax benefits. Try to consider as many of the above points as you can before prepaying your mortgage.

One final tip on mortgage prepayment. Never use companies that offer to set up a prepayment plan for you in the form of a biweekly payment schedule. There is a fee, usually $200 to $400, plus a monthly service charge. The advantage these companies tout is the built-in discipline to assure you make the payments. The disadvantage, of course, is that their fees eat up some of the savings you are trying to achieve by prepaying in the first place! Be your own disciplinarian; create your own prepayment plan, of whatever type you choose, and stick to it.

REVERSE **5** MORTGAGES

QUESTION: My wife and I are 68, and our house is paid for. We barely make ends meet on Social Security and have no extra funds for home repairs or emergencies. Would a reverse mortgage make sense?

ANSWER: Many seniors share similar circumstances—their largest asset, their home, is paid off or nearly paid off, but they are cash-strapped and unable to fully enjoy their retirement years. In the past, the only alternatives were to refinance the home, which is difficult unless the borrower can show the ability to make the payments, or to sell the home and move somewhere less expensive. A reverse mortgage presents a third possibility, but the first step is to consider alternatives. Reverse mortgages offer an interesting solution to the problems faced by many house-rich but cash-poor seniors. Reverse mortgages are fairly new products and thus, some explanation of the pros and cons is required.

A reverse mortgage is a loan against your home that you do
not have to pay back for as long as you live there. With a
reverse mortgage, you can turn the value of your home into
cash without having to move or to repay the loan each month.
The cash you get from a reverse mortgage can be paid to you
in several ways:

- all at once, in a single lump sum of cash;
- as a regular monthly cash advance;
- as a credit-line account that lets you decide when and
  how much of your available cash is paid to you; or
- as a combination of these payment methods

No matter how this loan is paid out to you, you typically do
not have to pay anything back until you die, sell your home,
or permanently move out of your home. To be eligible for
most reverse mortgages, you must own your home and be
62 years of age or older.

HOW REVERSE MORTGAGES WORK

To qualify for most loans, the lender checks your income to see how
much you can afford to pay back each month. But with a reverse
mortgage, you do not make monthly repayments. Therefore, you
don't need a minimum amount of income to qualify for a reverse
mortgage. In fact, you can have no income at all and still be able to
get a reverse mortgage.

With most home loans, you could lose your home if you do not
make your monthly payments. But with a reverse mortgage, there
aren't any monthly repayments to make. Most reverse mortgages
require no repayment for as long as you— or any co-owner(s)— live
in the home. Reverse mortgages differ from other home loans in
two important ways:

1. You don't need an income to qualify for a reverse mortgage;
   and
2. You don't have to make monthly repayments on a reverse
   mortgage.

Reverse Mortgages versus Forward Mortgages

The best way to see how a reverse mortgage works is by comparing it to a forward mortgage— the kind most people use to buy a home. Both types of mortgages create debt against your home. And both affect how much equity or ownership value you have in your home. But they do so in opposite ways.

Debt is the amount of money you owe a lender. It includes cash advances made to you or for your benefit, plus interest. Home equity means the value of your home (what it would sell for) minus any debt against it. For example, if your home is worth $150,000 and you still owe $30,000 on your mortgage, then your home equity is $120,000.

Forward Mortgages = Falling Debt, Rising Equity

When you purchased your home, you probably made a small down payment and borrowed the rest of the money you needed to buy it via your mortgage. Then you paid back your traditional forward mortgage loan every month over many years. During that time:

Your debt decreased,
and
Your home equity increased.

As you made each repayment, the amount you owed (your debt or loan balance) grew smaller. But your ownership value (your equity) grew larger. If you eventually made a final mortgage payment, you then owed nothing, and your home equity equaled the value of your home. In short, your forward mortgage was a falling debt, rising equity type of deal.

Reverse Mortgages = Rising Debt, Falling Equity

Reverse mortgages have the opposite purpose than forward mortgages. With a forward mortgage, you use your income to repay debt, and this builds up equity in your home. But with a reverse mortgage, you are taking the equity out in cash. So with a reverse mortgage:

Your debt increases,
and
Your home equity decreases.

In other words, it is just the opposite of a forward mortgage. With a reverse mortgage, the lender sends you cash, and you make no repayments. It feels like you are getting paid to live there whereas the reality is that you are being paid to eventually leave. So the amount you owe (your debt) gets larger as you get more and more cash and more interest is added to your loan balance. As your debt grows, your equity shrinks, unless your home's value is growing at an extremely high rate.

When a reverse mortgage becomes due and payable, you may owe a lot of money and your equity may be very small. If you have had the loan for a long time, or if your home has decreased in value over the life of the loan, there may not be any equity left at the end of the loan. Reverse mortgages are only for people who have a large percentage in equity and ultimately a time frame that allows for them to get paid their equity until they leave the home.

In short, a reverse mortgage is a rising debt, falling equity type of deal. But that is exactly what informed reverse mortgage borrowers want: to spend down their home equity while they live in their homes, without having to make monthly loan repayments.

Exception

As with everything, there is an exception. Reverse mortgages do not always have rising debt and falling equity. If a home's value grows rapidly, your equity could increase over time. Or, if you only get one loan advance and no interest is charged on it, your debt would never change. Therefore, your equity would grow as your home's value increases. However, most home values do not grow at consistently high rates, and interest is charged on most mortgages. So the majority of reverse mortgages do end up being rising debt, falling equity loans.

BASIC REVERSE LOAN FEATURES

Although there are different types of reverse mortgages, they are all similar in certain ways. Following are the features that most reverse loans have in common.

Homeownership

With a reverse mortgage, you remain the owner of your home just like when you had a forward mortgage. You are still responsible for paying your property taxes and homeowner's insurance and for making property repairs.

When the loan is over, you or your heirs must repay all of your cash advances plus interest. Reputable lenders do not want your house; they want repayment.

Financing Fees

You can use the money you get from a reverse mortgage to pay the various fees that are charged on the loan. This is called financing the loan costs. The costs are added to your loan balance and you pay them back, plus interest, when the loan is over.

Loan Amounts

The amount of money you can get depends most on the specific reverse mortgage plan or program you select. It also depends on the kind of cash advances you choose. Some reverse mortgages cost a lot more than others, and this reduces the amount of cash you can get from them.

Within each loan program, the amounts you can get generally depend on your age and your home's value:

* The older you are, the more cash you can get.
* The more your home is worth, the more cash you can get.

The specific dollar amount available to you may also depend on interest rates and closing costs on home loans in your area.

Debt Payoff

Generally, reverse mortgages must be first mortgages, meaning they must be the primary debt against your home. So if you currently owe any money on your property, you must either:

* pay off the old debt before you get a reverse mortgage; or
* pay off the old debt with the money you get from a reverse mortgage.

Most reverse mortgage borrowers pay off any home debt with a lump sum advance from their reverse mortgage. You might not have to pay off other debt against your home if the prior lender agrees to be repaid after the reverse mortgage is repaid. Generally only state or local government lending agencies are willing to consider subordinating their loans in this way.

The Debt You Take Is Equal to the Loan You Make

The debt you owe on a reverse mortgage equals all the loan advances you receive (including any you used to finance the loan or to pay off prior debt), plus all the interest that is added to your loan balance. If that amount is less than your home is worth when you pay back the loan, then you (or your estate) keep whatever amount is left over.

An estate is all assets owned by an individual at death, to be distributed according to the individual's will (or a court ruling if there is no will).

But if your rising loan balance ever grows to equal the value of your home, then your total debt is limited by the value of your home. To put it another way, you can never owe more than what your home is worth at the time the loan is repaid. The lender may not seek repayment from your income, your other assets, or from your heirs. Note: The technical term for this cap on your debt is a non-recourse limit. It means that the lender does not have legal recourse to anything other than your home's value when seeking repayment of the loan.

Payback

All reverse mortgages are due and payable when the last surviving borrower dies, sells the home, or permanently moves out of the home. A permanent move means that neither you nor any other coborrower has lived in your home for one continuous year.

Reverse mortgage lenders can also require repayment at any time if you:

- don't pay your property taxes;
- fail to maintain and repair the home; or
- don't keep your home insured.

These are fairly standard conditions of default on any mortgage. Always carefully read the paperwork you sign (not only is it wise, it is extremely helpful if you are battling a case of insomnia). On a reverse mortgage, however, lenders generally have the option to pay for these expenses by reducing your loan advances and using the difference to pay these obligations. This is only an option, however, if you have not already used up all your available loan funds.

Other default conditions on most home loans, including reverse mortgages, include:

- your declaration of bankruptcy;
- your donation or abandonment of your home;
- your perpetration of fraud or misrepresentation;
- if a government agency needs your property for public use (for example, to build a highway); or
- if a government agency condemns your property (for example, for health or safety reasons).

Remember: You can't change the rules in the middle of the game. There are changes that could affect the security of the loan for the lender and can therefore also make reverse mortgages payable. For example:

- renting out part or all of your home;
- adding a new owner to your home's title;
- changing your home's zoning classification; or
- taking out new debt against your home.

You must read the loan documents carefully to make certain you understand all the conditions that can cause your loan to become due.

COOLING OFF PERIOD: WANT TO CANCEL?

After closing a reverse mortgage, you have three days to reconsider your decision. If for any reason you decide you do not want the loan, you can cancel it. But you must do this within three business days after closing. Business days include Saturdays, but not Sundays or national holidays. Don't be ashamed to take advantage of this clause. Let's face it: Sometimes we change our minds and sometimes we get in over our heads. It would be best to thoroughly consider the consequences of a reverse mortgage before signing on the dotted line, but if you should find you have made a mistake, you have three days to rectify your financial future.

If you do decide to cancel, you must do it in writing using the form provided by the lender or by letter, fax, or telegram. Your notification must be hand delivered, mailed, faxed, or filed with a telegraph company before midnight of the third business day. You cannot cancel by telephone or in person. No e-mails either.

CONCLUSION

So there you have it: the good, the bad, and the ugly on homeownership. The more you know about available financial products, the better informed your home buying decisions will be. Don't be afraid to ask lenders, agents, and brokers questions about property history, confusing numbers, and that teeny tiny fine print. If someone doesn't take the time to explain something you don't understand, they aren't working for you. Make sure you fully comprehend everything about the paperwork you sign and the terms of your agreements. When it comes to home ownership, not educating yourself could be very costly.

RAISING FISCALLY RESPONSIBLE CHILDREN

When I was a child, I had dreams of how to make my millions. Unfortunately, most kids lack a clear concept of how to manage money, usually because no one has taken the time to teach them. The Joint Council on Economic Education examined youngsters' understanding of monetary concepts and found that kids, as a group, are appallingly ignorant. A majority of high school students, the council observed, "couldn't define *profit*." Yet, the *Wall Street Journal* noted that a New York retail consulting firm predicts that teenagers between the ages of 13 and 17 will spend $89 billion this year, with $34 billion of that amount coming from allowances. It seems clear that the only lesson most kids have learned about money is how to spend it. Learning to save it at an early age can be the difference between working until you're 50 or working until the day you die.

What accounts for this lack of financial education in our society? The financial snapshot in many households is horrendous, and lack of communication is usually the culprit. Most couples don't even communicate with one another about money so they certainly don't communicate with their children about this tricky yet very important topic. When it comes to money, what should be calm communication morphs into emotional anxiety. Often, money talk acts as a pawn in interpersonal conflicts, played as a source of manipulation or punishment. If you stop to analyze spousal fights that you have seen or experienced, they typically revolve around money or lack of communication about money. Parents are often at opposite poles and children sadly get caught in the cross fire, receiving mixed messages instead of good financial experience. The result? In order to avoid the emotional strain, most of us duck the chance to teach our kids how to manage money.

Yet the lessons we dread are simple. For kids, money management can be divided into basic lessons. The key to teaching kids is to start early using clear, practical examples. And, as your kids grow, so should the lessons and responsibilities.

KIDS AND MONEY

Children's interest in money coincides with their first urges to acquire some. Before that, money is simply something that spontaneously appeared in Mom's purse and was used to buy things. Once kids understand what money is, they want it. Children want to buy their own skateboard instead of having someone choose the wrong one. Although everyone will fret that this is the end of innocence, you should know that you cannot avoid this issue. Therefore, it is wise to instead seize this opportunity to raise money savvy kids.

Developing financial know-how requires practice and patience but above all, responsibility—not something kids learn overnight. But with practice, from growing bank accounts to handling grocery shopping, kids learn that handling money is more than just being helpful; they truly begin to understand the value of a buck.

KIDS AND ALLOWANCE

QUESTION: When does a child start getting an allowance?

ANSWER: Anybody old enough to spend money should get an allowance from the family funds. A good rule of thumb is by kindergarten, certainly by first grade.

Why give an allowance? For one big reason: to help your youngsters learn how to manage money. Let them learn what money is and how to count it. There are tons of great lessons to be realized via an allowance. An allowance is not given simply to relieve you of paying for some of your children's wants or needs. It is the best and most hands-on method of teaching your children how to spend and save. By using their own funds, their limits become real and tangible to them—they only get a certain amount each week, rather than having access to your seemingly infinite wallet. It will quickly become obvious that they can't have everything they want.

One of the biggest misconceptions about an allowance is that some parents cannot afford to give their children extra money. However, if you look at an allowance from a different angle, every parent *can* afford it. An allowance is basically money that you are going to spend on your child anyway, just given in a different form. Instead of paying for things at the time your children want them, you pay them an allowance and let them decide how to spend the money. The ultimate goal of an allowance is to teach children to distinguish between needs and wants and to prioritize and save—a difficult lesson that will be needed throughout their lives. Once you have decided to entrust your child with an allowance, it is time for the next hurdle—how much is enough?

How Much Allowance?

Obviously, you do not want your kids to be frustrated by too little allowance or overwhelmed by too much. To decide how much allowance is right for your particular family situation, consider several factors: the child's age, how much other kids in the area are getting, and where you live—kids in Iowa enjoy a lower cost of living than kids in New York or Los Angeles. Also consider your feelings with respect to responsibility; for how much of the total child's budget should he or she be held accountable? Also, how responsible a person is this particular child? Can he or she reasonably be expected to handle the sum you have in mind? Talk with friends who have children the same age and crunch the numbers. You can always make adjustments later.

EARNING MONEY

Having an adult's perspective on the matter, you know that there is a huge difference between being given money and actually earning

it. Kids don't automatically know this, and the only way for them to
learn is for them to experience it firsthand.

First Jobs

Once a kid finds out that the way he can get even more money is by
earning it, he exhibits an adrenaline rush that can transform a former couch spud into a mini dollar-crazy Hercules. Unfortunately,
the honeymoon can be short-lived unless you, the parent, help steer
your child toward appropriate jobs. Following are some tips.

Keep It Short

It is important that your child's first job have a distinct beginning
and end and won't last more than an hour or two. It should be
something like working alongside Grandpa filling leaf bags, wash-
ing his car, or shoveling his driveway. Perhaps you could delegate
tasks that you don't want to do but are within the grasp of your
child's abilities.

For a few bucks, your parents will get a little help and priceless
conversation, and the kids will earn some pocket change. Pocket
change sounds simple but it is a powerful enabler of financial
concept as I still remember most of the "dreams" that I saved up to
buy as a child. The jobs should be simple enough that soon the
children will be able to do the same jobs for people other than
their relatives.

Cultivating a Business

Making money means more than showing up for a job. Help turn a
chore into a business. Teach your child that doing regular chores is
like holding a job or running a business. During the summertime,
when the kids might want to expand their business, help them send
out flyers or place an ad. Although the ad will cost money, it will
likely bring in more jobs than the flyers and help their net profit.
Children will grasp this concept quickly. Have them negotiate with
the local paper to see if they offer a discount or even free ads for
kids. The kids will learn valuable lessons while reveling in the glory
of their newfound financial independence.

Limit Your Responsibility

Let's face it, if your kid takes on a job, you want to make sure they finish it or else you may be the one left holding the bag. So before you suggest your child start a job, try to assess how much you'll be responsible for if she can't complete it and be sure your child understands her responsibility. Don't be afraid to talk to your children and make sure they know the depth of the situation they are getting into.

Perseverance Pays

One job in particular that teaches perseverance is a paper route. A paper route is tough: The child has to deliver the paper in almost any weather, keep track of customers' bills, and because the base salary is low, he or she has to rely on tips from the customers.

Many times, children will question whether it's worth it. Encourage them to try it a bit longer; if they do a good job, customers will reward their efforts during the holidays. Most of the customers on the route usually will come through and help your children learn the value of persevering and a job well done.

New Frontiers

As your children get older, encourage them to explore more advanced work. Teenage children are perfect for baby-sitting, tutoring, or even being an assistant in a local computer class. As young children grow into their teen years, they must also learn the lesson of time management. Make sure your budding entrepreneur gets his homework done and studies for exams!

BEYOND THE PIGGY BANK: SAVING TECHNIQUES AND MOTIVATION

Once your children start earning money on a regular basis, help them save some of their earnings by opening a bank account. To encourage their savings habit, make a deal: You will deposit matching funds for any money they deposit and save for a one-year period.

Once this plan is working, consider taking advantage of savings vehicles that would earn them more interest. Focus on less risky and less complicated accounts, such as certificates of deposit (CDs). Show them how a few interest points will add up to a lot more money when compounded over time. Kids will be fascinated: The concept of money for nothing will not be lost on them!

What About Borrowing?

Sometimes the job money or the savings account won't be enough, and little Timmy will ask you for an advance on next week's allowance. Whether or not you should give an advance is a controversial subject. Beverly Tuttle, president of Consumer Credit Counseling Service of Connecticut, says, "It just invites the attitude that has made America a debt society: Buy now, pay later. It runs counter to the notion of planning."

On the other hand, life is unpredictable and you can't plan or save for everything. By giving an advance you can help teach your child about borrowing and interest. You heard correctly—I am suggesting that if you give your children a loan, you charge them interest, thereby teaching them how loans work and thus the pros and cons of debt.

Home Economics

Teaching kids to make and save money are important parts of being a responsible, fiscal citizen, but just as important is learning the relative value of money. Leaving light switches on when no one is in the room, turning up the heat in parts of the house that are not occupied—almost everything in life has a financial consequence.

Enlighten your children by getting them involved in running the household. Modern parenting can be so much fun! Set up an online checking account. If your child is computer literate, let them pay the bills electronically for the household. They will see it as an adult computer game; you will see it as a great opportunity to teach them about how much daily life costs, and perhaps improve their math skills with some bookkeeping.

At first you will worry if your children are old enough to be handling the family finances; obviously, you should carefully monitor their actions. For several months, work side-by-side systematically going through stacks of bills. Put a note on the statement and the amount that you want them to pay. Show them where to look for the account number on statements and where to record it both online and in a checkbook ledger. Practice makes perfect and it teaches kids valuable organizational skills. It won't take much time before they become adept at it.

After a few months, try to set up recurring payments (car, budgeted gas bill) on an automatic schedule, saving time and spreading expenditures over the year. But beyond balancing the budget, you will notice an additional benefit: Lights will be turned off and everyone in the family will be more conscious of how they spend their own money.

Responsible Splurging: Negotiating the Upgrade

Being fiscally responsible extends well beyond turning off light switches, especially when your kids start to get fashion conscious. Most people like to dress well, however, most people have to stick to a budget. Although you should be encouraging fiscal responsibility, try to understand your children's need for that occasionally unnecessary (or ridiculous) item—their feeling that "sometimes they just got to have it." Kids should be allowed the occasional splurge, just like grown ups!

For fashion conscious kids, you can address the issue of clothes by making a deal with your child: They might be allowed to "upgrade" to a higher-priced item, as long as they pay the difference between what was budgeted and the final price. That is where the allowance really kicks in and the idea of saving is endorsed. The child will feel good about how they look; they will whine less and save more; they will be happy and you will be happy.

DOLLAR-SENSE TIPS

- **Use specifics to make your point.** Next time you are buying gas, point out the continually running meter as the tank fills. Explain the process to your third grader: "Remember last Saturday? It took 11 gallons and cost $22.18. And then remember how we cut out some of those trips downtown this week? Because we drove less, it took only eight gallons when we filled the tank, and we saved more than $8." If your son or daughter actually participated in reducing your driving time over, say, a week, put some of the $8 you saved into his or her piggy bank.

- **Analyze allowance versus chores.** If you would normally pay an outsider for raking leaves or mowing the lawn, pay your child for doing the job instead. But don't set up dishwashing, bedmaking, or taking out the garbage as tasks that are payable by an allowance. These should be part of the normal household responsibilities shared by the family. The goal here is to teach money lessons—not to turn your children into paid servants!

- **Don't miss a payday.** Make the allowance as dependable as you expect your own paycheck to be—a regular amount on the same day each week. Never delay or miss a payment.

- **Don't use allowance to correct behavior.** If you need to hand out a punishment, never dock or withhold an allowance. That confuses both discipline and money-handling.

- **Help your child evaluate wants and needs.** Make sure your children understand, even on the simplest terms, that some of the allowance is for things they need, just as some is for wants. For example, steer your 7-year-old into the habit of regularly buying his own toothbrush. Since he's using his own money, let him pick the color or cartoon character. Though a minor diversion of money from household spending to the child's allowance, it helps establish the basis for a lifelong understanding of managing money to achieve a sound balance of needs and wants.

- **Remember, time is long when you're young.** If you are giving an advance on an allowance, don't stretch the repayment time. Two or three weeks are forever when you're eight or nine years old. Also remember that the younger the child, the shorter the time should be between starting to save and actually making the purchase—for preschoolers, just a few days. For older kids who want more expensive items, saving can and should stretch out longer.

THE COLLEGE YEARS

THE HARD REALITY OF TUITION COSTS

The headline in the morning paper says it all: "Tuition Devouring More of Family Income." It seems that tuition costs aren't just rising steadily, like a financial iceberg that we will inevitably hit. They are also responsible for a huge, gaping hole in the typical family income, more than anyone previously realized. And, the less a family earns, the harder they'll get hit. College costs are becoming more and more of a nightmare for the American family.

A study by the National Center for Public Policy and Higher Education found that for families at or near the bottom of the income ladder, tuition at public colleges and universities equaled 25 percent of income, up from 13 percent in 1980. The richest 20 percent of American families, meanwhile, continued to spend just 2 percent of their income on tuition, with no change over the past 20 years. During the same time period, tuition costs at state schools rose 107 percent, when adjusted for inflation. These are crazy statistics, but telling all the same.

Rather than ignore the looming reality or prepare to drown in a sea of debt, financial planners suggest that parents become savvy savers and start making use of the growing number of options designed to finance a child's education.

How Much Will College Cost?

Ultimately, how much you spend depends on what type of school your child attends. As a general rule, private colleges and universities are two to four times more expensive than state schools. And while it is difficult to know exactly how much tuition fees will be years from now, experts project rapid yearly increases. Between 2001 and 2002, for instance, tuition and fees rose 5.8 percent at four-year private colleges (to an annual average cost of $18,273) and 9.6 percent at four-year public colleges (to an annual average cost of $4,081).[1]

But before you freak out, consider this:

- College is still a good investment in your child's future. People with four-year degrees earn 80 percent more on average than those with high school diplomas, according to the U.S. Census Bureau. That can add up to more than a million dollars in additional income over a lifetime.
- Most students attend affordable colleges. Almost 70 percent of students enrolled in four-year schools in 2002 paid less than $8,000 a year for tuition.
- In 2002, only 7 percent of all students attended extremely expensive schools (tuition over $24,000).
- Financial aid is available for most students. More than 75 percent of students in private schools and 60 percent in public schools receive some type of financial aid.

BEST WAYS TO SAVE FOR COLLEGE

Following is a quick overview of the most popular ways to save for college.

---

[1]According to the Non-Profit College Board

529 College Savings Plans

A 529 college savings plan is an investment account that allows you to set aside money for your child's education and let it grow tax free. The federal government won't tax your money when you take it out of the account as long as it is used for higher education. Any family can contribute to a 529 account regardless of income, and there is a lifetime maximum contribution of roughly $290,000 (this varies from state to state). The best part: You can often start an account with as little as $25, and you can use the money in a 529 plan at any accredited college or university in the country.

Prepaid Tuition Plans

Prepaid tuition plans are investment accounts that allow you to pay for your child's future college tuition (or a portion of it) at today's prices. If you have enough money now, you could pay for a complete four-year degree that your child won't use for another 18 years. Or, if your budget is more modest, you can prepay a portion of your child's college expenses. Prepaid tuition plans are administered by individual states and most can only be redeemed at public colleges and universities in that state. In many cases, you or the student beneficiary of the account must also live in that state.

Coverdell Education Savings Account

A Coverdell account functions very much like an IRA but for education, not retirement purposes. You make a contribution of up to $2,000 per year (with post-tax dollars), the money grows tax-free, and neither the contribution nor the interest is taxed when you make a withdrawal, as long as you use it for education purposes.

Custodial Accounts

In very basic terms, a custodial account is a savings account in your child's name that you control (if you are the custodian) until he reaches legal adulthood (18 to 21, depending on where you live). You make the decisions about how much to put into the account, how the money is invested, how earnings are reinvested, and when to take money out of the account to spend on your child's behalf.

You can deposit cash, savings bonds, and other securities in a custodial account. The first $750 of earnings each year are tax free, and the next $750 of earnings are taxed annually at your child's rate—generally 15 percent. Any earnings beyond that are taxed at your rate. Withdrawals are subject to federal tax as well.

IRA and Roth IRA accounts

Traditional and Roth IRAs are both investment accounts that allow you to save money for retirement or college while avoiding significant taxes. That's right! You can save money for your child's college at the same time you are saving for your retirement. Traditional IRAs come in two forms—deductible and nondeductible. Your eligibility for a traditional deductible IRA depends on your income and whether your employer has a retirement plan. In a deductible IRA your annual contributions are tax deductible, but when you withdraw money from the account, you'll be taxed on both your contributions and your earnings. In a Roth IRA, your contributions are not tax deductible, but your earnings are tax-free if you withdraw them after the required five-year holding period and use the money for qualified expenses such as college tuition.

QUESTIONS AND ANSWERS ABOUT COLLEGE SAVINGS

QUESTION: My parents would like to give us money to start a college fund for our child. Whose name should we put the money in, and how should we invest it?

ANSWER: A 529 college savings plan is the best place to start. It has advantages for your parents and your child. This type of account can help you avoid gift taxes and also prevent your child from losing out on future financial aid.

Most families set up 529 accounts with the parents as the owners and the child as the beneficiary. With this arrangement, when it comes time to calculate financial aid, the child has "5.6 percent visibility." That means that 5.6 percent of the money in the 529 account will be factored in to your child's financial aid calculations as an asset, thereby reducing your child's need.

HOT TIP

Set up the 529 account so that your parents are the owners
and your child is the beneficiary. Both you and your parents
can contribute to the account, and all of you can get the federal and state tax deductions. But if the grandparents are the
owners of the account, it is invisible on most college financial
aid forms. It depends on the school, of course, but most
schools do not require your child to list money that is owned
by his grandparents, even though he or she is the beneficiary.

---

529 plans have other advantages too. Your parents can make
contributions of up to $11,000 per year free of gift and estate taxes.
If they want to give more, they can make a one-time gift of up to
$55,000 tax-free, provided they don't make any other contributions
over the next five years.

The maximum contribution levels for 529 plans vary by state,
but most are quite high (between $125,000 and $250,000), so
chances are your parents can continue their generous support of
your child's education over the years without reaching the limit.

QUESTION: I have two kids: an infant and a 3-year-old. What is the
best way to save for their college education? I currently have a savings account for my 3-year-old, but I feel that I could do better.

ANSWER: Increases in college tuition routinely outstrip increases in
inflation. A savings account will struggle to keep pace with inflation
and isn't a very attractive investment vehicle for your children's
college fund.

Think about more than just setting money aside. Think about
how the investment returns are taxed, how investment returns have
to outpace rising costs to see an increase in your purchasing power,
the annual expenses of investing in different plans, and how different
plans will influence your child's ability to qualify for financial aid.

Savingforcollege.com is a great Internet resource, rating the
various Section 529 plans and providing an overview of tax, gift, and
account control issues for several college savings plans.

So much of preparing for college depends on your personal
finances, if and where your children decide to go to college, and

your state's income tax code—there is no definitive answer about which plan to choose. Investing in your children's future, however, is always a winning proposition. If you look at your options but are still not able to decide, then consult a tax professional to help you make a decision.

QUESTION: What do you think about the Upromise College saving plan?

ANSWER: Several affinity programs have sprung up to help parents find everyday ways to put money in their Section 529 college savings plans. Upromise is one such plan, BabyMint is another. Upromise is the larger of the two; both are reputable.

Registering your credit cards, using affiliated merchants, or both earns you points that translate into contributions to a college savings plan account. The money can later be withdrawn tax-free from a Section 529 account when used for qualified education expenses. You can also get friends and relatives to set up accounts that can be used to finance your children's college expenses.

In addition to these plans, several individual credit card companies and financial institutions have set up similar plans: Buy a quart of milk with your credit card, and a few pennies go into your 529 account. MBNA, Visa, and Fidelity are among the institutions that are involved in such offers for some 529 plans.

My concern isn't that the firms are not trustworthy (they are), since the money is being put into your college savings plan account; it's that consumers stop making good purchase decisions because they get caught up in the idea that they're earning points for the children's college fund.

We've all heard stories about how people have altered their behavior or travel plans to earn frequent flier miles. People will buy a $3,000 couch in order to get a $300 flight. Affinity programs try to build loyalty and influence behavior to increase business for the firms affiliated with the program. There is nothing wrong with that, as long as you understand and manage the process. But if you end up spending an extra 10 percent on a purchase to earn 4 percent in points, you have lost money.

Another thing you must consider is that you are making a lot of your transaction information available to these companies. You need to be aware of how that information might be used. I personally am not stressed about this but that said, I do have a paper shredder. Be safe; you really need to read the privacy policy, agree to its provisions, and be aware of any changes to that policy over time.

Also, do not be fooled. Spending to accumulate college savings is a much longer path to reaching your financial goal than simply establishing a college savings program. Spending $40 on a dinner out may put $2 in a college savings account, but spending $8 on dinner at home allows you to invest the $32 difference. Be smart about your savings! Make sure you plan for the total cost of college and don't just rely on Upromise or a 529 plan as the only funding for your child's college costs.

Think of these programs as the frosting, not the cake, in funding your children's college expenses. Although it may provide a boost, this shouldn't be your only plan.

QUESTION: Even though college costs will be enormous, you still should save for retirement first, right?

ANSWER: Absolutely true in 10-foot capital letters! You can borrow for college. You cannot borrow for retirement. College lasts four years; retirement lasts much longer. Retirement always comes first!

Another reason is this: College is typically an investment that returns higher income in the future, through children's increased earnings. A retirement fund can also be used as an emergency fund for college. If you have an IRA, you can withdraw money for college without incurring the premature withdrawal penalty. That has been true since 1997.

QUESTION: We are a young couple just getting established. Does it make more sense to sock money into a 401(k) account, or split savings between a 401(k) retirement plan and a 529 (state-run college savings plan)?

ANSWER: For most people, the answer is to put it in a 401(k), especially if your employer is participating in a matching program. I hate to be the one to say this but I have to: Sometimes your children don't turn out like you want them to and in that case you don't want to be retirement poor while funding your child's 8-year college plan.

QUESTION: What about the theory, "The fewer assets I have, the more financial aid my child will receive"?

ANSWER: Truth be told, financial aid formulas are more income-intense than asset-intense. If the focus is on earning need-based aid, you need to find ways to reduce your income. The more you transfer income to assets, the better, in the years prior to filing your financial aid application.

That's the way the system is geared right now. It does reward families that spend now, save later. But if you have the dollars, you are going to have more choices when it comes to a school. You aren't going to have to limit your child to following the aid dollars. Another consideration is that financial aid changes all the time. The way the rules work right now may not be the way they work in 15 years when your child goes to college.

QUESTION: My question is about 529 plans. If I want my son to go to the University of California, do I have to put my money into the California plan when Nebraska's has a better rate of return?

ANSWER: Not at all. This is confusing but you can put your money into any state plan and use it essentially for any accredited college or university. In fact, there may or may not be any incentive to put money into your own state's plan. A lot of states do provide incentives, such as up-front tax deductions for contributions, or beneficial treatment of accounts in determining eligibility for state financial aid programs. New York does this; it doesn't count the money invested in the state's 529 plan as an asset. Some states, including Minnesota, Louisiana, and Michigan, actually offer matching contributions for families below certain income levels.

QUESTION: What's the difference between a 529 plan and a Coverdell Education Savings Account?

ANSWER: The Coverdell can be withdrawn tax-free not just for college, but also for K through 12 education expenses—anything from tutoring and tuition to books and home computers. You are limited to contributing $2,000 per year per child, whereas there are no annual limits with the 529. Each 529 plan established its own overall account-balance limit; the highest right now is $305,000 in South Dakota. The Coverdell has age limits on the beneficiary—he or she must be under 18—and the account must be used by the time the beneficiary is age 30. With a 529, you can set aside money to return to graduate school yourself. With the 529, the state handles investment options. With the Coverdell, you do.

Also, a Coverdell is a child's asset. When I work with families that want their children to attend private school, I advise them to use the Coverdell for tax-advantaged money for the elementary and high school years, and a 529 plan for college.

QUESTION: What about prepaid tuition plans?

ANSWER: Generally they are very good for citizens of that state, if the child is likely to stay in the state to go to school. The prepaid plan can be a very good place to have your money if there are double-digit inflation increases in your state colleges, which we are seeing at public institutions across the country. But there are big restrictions and limitations from state to state. Check Saving forcollege.com to see if your state offers a prepaid tuition program.

QUESTION: What if I can't save anything for college, because I'm spending my education dollars on private school tuition or tutoring now?

ANSWER: That's a tough situation. Most families can't afford private school, elite colleges, and a comfortable retirement. This is one of those situations where you have to sit down, run the numbers, and set realistic expectations.

Be it private school or tutoring, music lessons or summer opportunities—all of these are enrichments that make a child more attractive to an institution, not to mention the personal benefits for the child. But applications at highly selective colleges are also carefully read and put into context.

QUESTION: What's the best "saving for college" advice if you have a baby?

ANSWER: If you have a qualified retirement plan, that's your first choice. Seriously, take care of your retirement as I can not stress enough that you can pay for school out of this fund but once you are retired, your child may not take care of you. As cliché as it sounds, pay your self first. Decide what you're going to save and where you're going to save it, and build your budget around what's left after you have made savings deposits. Remember that you can always pay for the child's college through loans, scholarships, and grants. If those are not options then you can tap into your 401(k) or retirement vehicle. Saving for college in a child's name does not make sense if you are going to ignore your own financial condition.

QUESTION: What's the best "saving for college" advice if you have a 10-year-old?

ANSWER: Look at how you are investing. At this age you may be more accepting of risk because dips in the market are likely to be averaged out with bull markets. A lot of 529 plans have strategies that automatically change the asset allocation as the child gets older. A 5-year-old has more time to be exposed to risk and even a 10-year-old has eight plus years to be exposed to market fluctuations. The market goes up historically seven out of ten years so don't be too conservative and nervous.

QUESTION: What's the best "saving for college" advice if you have a 15-year-old?

ANSWER: If you have a teen and haven't saved anything, it's time to readjust your life and start living as if you're making tuition payments right now. Pretend your child is going to college next year. Using your income today, see what families are expected to contribute at a college of your choice. That's your savings target. You don't have a lot of choices other than to be realistic. Don't try to hit a home run with the little savings that you do have.

QUESTION: What's bad advice about college savings?

ANSWER: Bad advice?! Don't plan for your kids' college! Seriously, the most frequent discussion has to do with assets in the child's name. I already mentioned that your children may not turn out like you dreamed they would. It happens! Also the federal assessment formula for student assets is 35 percent, and some institutions use 25 percent, so it is five to seven times the rate it would be if it were in the parent's name.

Beware of jumping into a 529 plan if a financial professional tells you, "Buy this state's plan" but at the same time they won't tell you about any of the others. I've heard it said that 20 percent of young people don't go beyond freshman year. So if you save for four years of college in a restricted plan without other children to name as a beneficiary, then you have to pay income tax rather than capital gains, plus a penalty in order to get your own money back. Make sure you understand the ins and outs of your college savings vehicle. Ask questions.

QUESTION: Should I assume as a parent, that when my child is accepted to college I'll be able to talk the financial aid officer into giving me more aid, or matching another school's offer?

ANSWER: Ha! Don't count on it. Schools are increasingly unable to negotiate offers and you have no way of knowing what the situation will be in the year that your child will apply. Simply asking for more money doesn't necessarily mean you'll get it. With that said, please do explore all financial aid options as I personally got four years of college grants for which I never thought I would qualify.

Those institutions that give need-based aid, such as the Ivy Leagues, are going to use a formula based on family resources to provide aid equal to full need. Still others have merit-based aid programs. Brandishing a letter from another institution that also awards aid on the basis of need, but that measured the aid in a different way, *might* cause the Admissions Board to say, "Hmm, let's look it over again and perhaps have an interview with the family." It happens. But the majority of institutions in the United States can not meet your full need because their resources are limited.

THE FINANCIAL REALITIES OF RETIREMENT

WORRYING ABOUT MONEY PERSISTS IN RETIREMENT

Of all retirees, approximately one-quarter (24 percent) have little confidence and almost half (43 percent) are only somewhat confident that they will have enough money to live comfortably in retirement.

Preretirees Are Unprepared

Nearly two-thirds of those who have not yet reached retirement age (61 percent) have not calculated how much money they will need to save by the time they retire. Of those that have done the calculation, 36 percent do not know or remember how much they will need to save by the time they retire.

Time Is Running Out

Most people would like the timing of their retirement to be their choice. However, most leave their jobs for unexpected reasons such as health problems or disability (50 percent) or changes within their company, such as downsizing or closure (23 percent).

POPULATION GROWTH AND SOCIAL SECURITY

Between 2010 and 2030, the size of the 65+ population will grow by more than 75 percent, while the population paying payroll (Social Security) taxes will rise less than 5 percent. Social Security benefits make up 50 percent of the average retiree's income.[1]

America Is Growing Older

America is graying and take note because this means the country will change its spending habits. Today, one in eight Americans is aged 65 or older. As the first wave of the baby boom generation begins to retire after 2010 (early retirement for Social Security benefits would occur in 2008), the share of older Americans will increase significantly. By 2040, nearly one in four will be 65 or older. At the same time, life expectancy will continue to rise. On average, Americans are living 14 years longer than when Social Security was created, and the trend towards a longer lifespan will continue. These demographic changes will place tremendous fiscal pressure on federal retirement and health programs for the elderly. Furthermore, a baby bust succeeded the baby boom, meaning that there will be fewer workers to help finance each retiree's benefits in the future.

Secure Your Retirement

Laying the foundation for economic growth in the face of profound demographic changes is perhaps the most difficult challenge facing the United States. The imminent retirement of the baby boom generation, combined with longer life expectancies will place enor-

---

[1]Source: http://www.principal.com/wellbeing/global, *The Principal Global Financial Well-Being Study*, 2004.

mous pressure on the economic resources. These resources have become necessary to sustain the rising standard of living that Americans have come to expect. The burden of an aging America could potentially fray the threads of the safety net programs the government provides for senior citizens.

For most Americans, a secure retirement means retaining a comfortable standard of living through retirement—from the first day of retirement to the very last. That requires a steady stream of income that, combined with Social Security and other retirement income, covers basic living expenses—from rent to doctor's bills, taxes to transportation, food to clothing.

What most Americans want is a guaranteed retirement paycheck for life. Get real! Think you can count on Social Security to cover your current life style in retirement? Think again.

We Have Promised Too Much

I took a college class on welfare and the one thing that I learned is that there are no right answers. Federal entitlement programs—under which money is spent automatically on a category of recipients who meet government-specified qualifications—consume an ever-increasing share of our country's financial resources. Spending on entitlements (principally federal health and retirement programs) has more than doubled since 1963 and now accounts for almost half of federal outlays. By the government's own estimates, at the current rate of federal spending entitlements could absorb all government revenues by 2030.

Americans Are Saving Too Little

As a country and as individuals, we are not saving enough to meet our future needs. This has crisis written all over it and yet no one is willing to discuss this out loud and in public. The rate of personal savings has declined steadily over the past few decades and now is approaching historic lows—insufficient to meet the future retirement needs of most Americans. Although recent gains in financial markets have buoyed a sense of wealth in many Americans, current annual individual savings rates are near zero. In fact, Americans, as a whole, actually had negative savings rates (as a percentage of disposable income) for the months September and October 1998.

According to the U.S. Department of Commerce, this constitutes the first negative monthly national savings rates since the agency began keeping such statistics more than 40 years ago. Low savings not only threatens the ability of individuals to retire with financial security, it also reduces the pool of capital available for investment, the pool that creates jobs and economic growth—all essential elements of higher standards of living for all Americans.

These Trends Are Unsustainable

Without significant public policy and social responses to the impending challenges, the standard of living for retirees after the first quarter of the twenty-first century will likely decline. Society will be unable to afford all the promises we have made. Seniors will be forced into decisions that are less than honorable—which will they choose, food or prescription drugs? A failure to act boldly with structural reforms now will raise future costs dramatically and require added sacrifices 10 to 20 years down the road. Policymakers who have examined the issue recognize both the need for action and the benefits of acting sooner rather than later.

The Social Safety Net

Presently, inflows to the Social Security system exceed benefits paid out. This is nothing new to anyone who stays on top of the news. The program's trust fund will begin to pay out more in benefits than it collects in payroll taxes soon after the baby boomers begin retiring, however, and will run even larger annual operating deficits thereafter. According to the Social Security trustees, if no action is taken in the interim, the trust fund will be entirely depleted by 2032. Because of these trends, polls show young people are losing faith in the system. Personally, I don't feel that anyone should count on Social Security offering them anything if they are 30 or younger. The system is indeed that broken, so take care of yourself; otherwise, retirement might not be pretty.

Private Retirement Plans

Currently, fewer than half of all workers are enrolled in an employer-sponsored pension plan. The problem is even more acute for those working in small businesses. As of 1993, 84 percent of workers in companies employing more than 1,000 people had access to a retirement plan, but only 17 percent of workers in companies with 25 or fewer employees had a retirement plan available to them at work. As a result, only about 20 percent of Americans in businesses with 100 or fewer employees participate in a retirement plan. The problem is worse for women and minorities who tend to have shorter job tenures and who are more likely to be part-time employees without coverage by an employer-sponsored plan. Don't even get me started about how short-shifted women are in the United States when it comes to retirement planning. Women tend to take off time early in their careers to raise children and then do it again to take care of their aging husbands because men tend to die before women. All that time off means less money saved. Clearly, women need to plan differently than men do.

Personal Savings

As they do now, future retirees must supplement Social Security payments with personal savings. Financial experts tell us, however, that current levels of personal retirement savings are not nearly enough to ensure financial independence for retirement—even *with* pension and Social Security payments. The rate of personal savings fell from almost 12 percent of gross domestic product (GDP) in 1965 to about 5 percent of GDP in 1995 and has continued to decline. According to one study by Merrill Lynch, the oldest baby boomers are saving just one-third of what they will need to maintain their current standard of living during retirement. The cold hard truth is that most American families have very little set aside to meet future retirement expenses.

Avoid Variable Annuities

Lately, I see too many conservative investors flocking to variable annuities. Insurance salesmen sell this product with misleading information, whereas the truth of the matter is almost black and white and is written into the contracts "investors" are signing. But as I see it, sales ought to be slumping and the only buyers should be young cheapskates and graying gamblers.

Okay, this will take a little explaining.

Variable annuities offer the chance to get tax-deferred growth by investing in a menu of mutual funds. Wrapped into that package is insurance that ensures your heirs will get more than the account's current value, should you have the misfortune to both die and also fare poorly with your investments.

According to the National Association for Variable Annuities in Reston, Virginia, these oddball investments pulled in a net $13.2 billion in 2003's third quarter, the latest period for which data are available. That was up from $8.1 billion a year earlier.

Yet, if anything, variable annuity sales ought to be drying up. Why? For starters, the 2003 tax law dented their allure, by making taxable account investing more attractive.

Sure, a variable annuity gives you tax-deferred growth. But withdrawals are taxed as ordinary income, which means you could lose as much as 35 percent to Uncle Sam. By contrast, if you invest through a taxable account, your dividends and long-term capital gains are now dunned at a maximum 15 percent. By all rights, the change in capital gains and dividend tax rates should have gutted sales of these things.

Even before 2004 tax law changes, variable annuities were a dubious proposition. According to Chicago's Morningstar, if you buy stock and bond funds through a variable annuity, you will pay average annual expenses equal to a hefty 2.28 percent of assets. A big reason for this high cost is the 1.18 percent average "mortality and expense" charge. This insurance guarantees a minimum death benefit. Some variable annuities simply promise that your heirs will get back the amount you invested, in the unlikely event you lose money on the account during your lifetime.

Other death benefits are more generous. For instance, some variable annuities promise that your heirs will get back at least the amount you invested plus maybe 5 percent or 7 percent in annual interest. Others will pay your heirs the account's "highest value," with that high value determined as of a particular date each year. These rising death benefits might cap out at, say, age 80, and they will be reduced if you withdraw money from the annuity.

Time for Change

Weakness in the Social Security program combined with lack of pension coverage for half of the labor force means that workers place a greater reliance on their own retirement savings to cover these gaps. Yet, despite these potential shortfalls, personal savings rates continue to hover at historically low levels. This has to change. Current economic uncertainties may exacerbate this trend, threatening the prospects for individuals' future retirement income. Taking this information to a personal level, where are you going to be when you're too old to support yourself? What's going to happen to you?

The good news is that Congress can help. Though Congress is correctly doing much to encourage saving for retirement, there are not sufficient incentives in place today to support the types of retirement vehicles that will pay retirees a steady paycheck for life and help them manage their retirement savings.

INVESTING FOR LIFE

The economy has just emerged from a time unlike any other. Twenty years ago, stocks were an incredible investment. People made millions simply by buying stocks. The stock market has made more millionaires than any company or companies will ever make. It was a bonanza for those who owned them and a letdown for those who sold them too early. And then it was over: The market corrected heavily between 2000 and 2003. Investors relearned a monumental, painful lesson that human beings have known for millennia: Don't put all your eggs in one basket. There are investments other than stocks. And this book is going to cover them. Not only will you learn about assets like stocks, bonds, cash, and real estate, but you'll also learn about other strategies that will safely maneuver you toward retirement.

I am not presuming that the next several chapters will comprise everything you will ever need to know about investing, but it will be a healthy start. You deserve a chance to capitalize on the various forms of attaining wealth that are out there, and I want you to be confident and informed. I will tell you everything I know about gaining financial freedom via investing. But the rest is up to you.

How to Invest

How are you going to choose from the 100 plus financial services companies that offer investing services? This really is not an easy choice and on a daily basis I see people all over the map on the direction they choose. You can choose from among discount brokerages, deep discount brokerages, full-service firms, banks, and mutual fund companies.

There are "online only" firms who conduct business solely through the Internet and phone. There are "click and mortar" firms like Schwab and Quick & Reilly who offer both Internet trading and have a network of branch offices across the country. Some of the online only firms are building real-world presence, such as E*Trade, who has formed a partnership to put investment centers inside Target Stores. Some firms, like E*Trade, offer banking and other financial services. Some, like Ameritrade, focus only on the core business of investment transactions.

The bigger online brokerages, such as Schwab, Fidelity, and E*Trade, need to be everything to everybody (at least as much as is possible). Some will focus on catering to rapid-fire day traders. Some will brand themselves as cheap, some as fast, some as reliable, some as having fine customer service, some as having the best research available. Some are established and some are new. All of them are trying to compete for your business.

Let's begin your new life of healthy investing right now. Your job is to find an online broker that best meets your needs. Give this task the same consideration you would give to choosing a new business partner. You have many, many choices, and that sometimes makes it hard to decide, but I'll present a few ideas and a few tools to help you along.

STEP ONE:
WHAT TYPE OF ACCOUNT TO OPEN

IT'S ALL ABOUT YOU (CHECKLIST)

You'll find plenty of opinions about who are the best/worst online brokerage firms, but only one person's opinion actually counts, and that's yours. Start by taking inventory and asking yourself what you really want to do, what you have to work with, and what you want to get out of investing online. Ask yourself:

* Do you intend to buy and hold and build capital appreciation while saving some money on the trades? Or do you

intend to trade frequently, locking in small profits, holding positions for only weeks, days, or even hours? Will you do some of each?

- Are you looking for one place to consolidate all your financial activity? Would you rather work with a firm that specializes in online trading?
- Do you want to be able to buy a stock then send the money later, or will you be content to have the money in an account so that the payment is made instantaneously when you place the trade?
- How important to you is access to customer service? Will you want 24/7 support, or are Monday through Friday business hours good enough? Would it be beneficial to you to have a branch office nearby? If you travel, do you prefer a firm with branches nationwide?
- How much money do you have to start with? Can you meet the minimum opening balance? If you need to start small, that will limit your choices. Some firms charge a maintenance fee for low-balance and low-activity accounts. On the other hand, if you've got a relatively high net worth or you trade frequently, some firms provide premium services to very active traders and high net worth investors.
- How much do you value stability and history? Would you rather go with an established firm, or would you be willing to go with a relatively unknown and fairly new company?
- Will you use your own financial software, such as Quicken or Microsoft Money?
- Will your online broker support easy downloads to those software programs?
- Would you also like to have multiple means of access? I don't just mean using the Internet from a PC. What about trading with a live broker, by touch-tone phone system, by wireless devices such as a PDA, or by fax? Some firms offer a trading software platform, which may have advantages over Web-based trading.

These are just a few of the things to think about while selecting a broker. Every brokerage firm has its own policies, and if you are seriously looking at doing business with one, you'll need to know the policies ahead of time. Don't make assumptions. Find the answers by going to the company's Web sites and asking customer service reps. I have a list of questions you may consider asking a brokerage firm before you sign up with them, provided on pages 94–96 of this book.

And the Winner Is: Using "Best Of" Lists

The good news is, whenever there's a difficult choice to be made, there is usually someone who makes a living by helping you make an informed choice. There are a number of consumer, financial, and computer publications that regularly review online brokerage firms and offer their considered opinion as to which are best. I suggest hitting Google and doing some searches.

Unfortunately the research doesn't always make the choice easier. When I go online, I have no problem finding well-considered opinions, but I can't find much in the way of consensus. One reviewer rates a firm as top-notch, but another puts that firm in the middle of the pack. Reviewers all analyze the same firms, study the same fee schedules, and learn of each firm's policies and products, yet they come up with distinctly different opinions. Why is that?

The difference, of course, is in the methodology used to collect and interpret the data. Each reviewer puts his or her own weighting on each criterion under review. Everyone agrees that cost, speed, service, quality executions, and range of products are important, but just how important each one is relative to the whole is rather subjective. For example, all reviewers rate commissions, and agree that cheaper is generally better.

However, most reviewers give a rather low priority to commissions and fees, so it's a relatively small part of the overall equation. That doesn't mean fees aren't important, just that reviewers generally feel that other aspects are more important.

Of course if you're just out for the cheapest trade possible, then expert reviews may not be all that useful to you, simply because you put a greater emphasis on costs than they do. If you are just looking for the cheapest trade, I would suggest that you use an expert review to help you sort through other criteria. Among those offering the lowest fees, you might want to see which ones are rated best for speed and execution quality because a slow response or poor execution can cost you far more than the difference in commission.

The people who create these lists have to meet the needs of the broadest possible range of their readership. That doesn't necessarily mean that what they think is best overall is best for you. I met a reviewer for a major financial publication, and he uses a brokerage that didn't make it to his own "best of" list. Why? The firm he uses meets his individual needs just fine, and he didn't need the services of the others, even though he rated them as excellent. He said, "If you are happy with the company you work with, there is no need to change."

So don't be concerned if your brokerage firm got a bad review, as long as you're satisfied. This industry changes quickly, and so do the "best of" lists. The firm that got low marks for having a cluttered and confusing Web site gets a makeover. The one that scored high praise for a fast and responsive network now finds itself overloaded.

Another that got low marks for speed six months ago invested in new hardware and doubled its capacity. And that is the magic of the marketplace.

If you change brokers every time the "top ten" list changes, you'll spend more time moving your money than investing it.

DOING YOUR OWN EVALUATION

A "best of" list can help guide you, but you ultimately must decide for yourself. Again, only your opinion matters, and here are some of my tips for helping you create an informed opinion. Of course these tips are just my opinions, so take them for what they are. Quick note: A brokerage firm is also called a broker-dealer, so I'll use that term as well. I'll use the word broker to mean a person who works for a broker-dealer.

Bright Blue Sky

This is unlikely to be a problem, but you do have to know if the broker-dealer is licensed to do business in your state of residence. If not, scratch it off your list, as you can not open an account with that firm. Every state has blue-sky laws designed to protect the people who live in that state from securities fraud (and end up being sold "nothing but blue sky").

The Company You Keep

Is the broker-dealer a member of the National Association of Securities Dealers (NASD) or of the New York Stock Exchange (NYSE)? NASD membership is pretty much essential. NYSE membership is highly desirable, much like the Good Housekeeping Seal of Approval. In my research, I've not come across a broker-dealer that was not an NASD member, but not all are NYSE members.

Insurable Interest

Just like banks have FDIC insurance against failure, the securities industry has an insurance program called the Security Investor Protection Corporation (SIPC). SIPC member firms pay into an insurance pool to safeguard investors against failure and insolvency of a broker-dealer. That way, if the firm goes bankrupt, your investments don't go down along with it. SIPC protection will insure each customer up to $500,000 and up to $100,000 of that claim can be cash. Money market funds are not cash, so they're not affected by the $100,000 limit.

Many firms also carry private insurance above the SIPC coverage. Insurance carriers like Aetna may offer $1 million to $10 million worth of protection per account. Sure, most of us won't need that kind of coverage, but it's nice to know it's there.

How likely is a broker-dealer to fail and go bankrupt? Good question. Fortunately, failure rates have been very low. A floundering firm is far more likely to merge or get bought out by a larger and more stable firm. Online brokerages have to spend a lot of money to acquire new clients, so it might be cheaper to buy out an existing firm and all its clients than to try and get new ones.

But nothing's impossible, and if it comes down to it, the SIPC will oversee the process of making the firm's clients whole again. Wherever possible, the SIPC will convert shares held with your brokerage firm (in "street name") to paper certificates and mail them to you. Otherwise, the SIPC appoints a custodial firm and transfers your assets there. You may elect to stay with that broker or transfer your shares to another. Most investors are made whole in one to three months.

Take the Brokerage for a Test Drive

Most of the brokerages have demos on their sites, but some give you a better idea of what they're really like than others. While you are investigating brokerages, start by going to their home page and look for a link marked demo or something like that. Spend some time here; it's worth the effort. Even if you have had very little experience with online investing, by the time you've looked at about four to six of them, you will probably develop a sense of what you like and what you don't like.

Customer Service

Investing is largely self-service, and you are reading this book to help you become more independent, but from time to time you will need the help of a broker or a customer service representative. Some firms have phone lines open round-the-clock and are never closed. Some will be available only during market hours and will be closed nights and weekends. How important are access hours to you? Some people can only tend to their personal finances on nights and weekends, so a Monday to Friday firm may not be much help to them. The deeper discount firms tend to keep shorter hours, so you may face a trade-off between price and service hours.

Of course you won't do all of your business over the phone. When you trade online, you will often use e-mail to reach customer service. Try to find out your firm's stated e-mail turnaround policy: 24 to 48 hours for a personalized response is pretty standard. Some firms have an auto-reply system, so when you send them an e-mail, their computer sends you an e-mail to tell you it was received and someone will reply within a specified time frame.

STEP TWO:
GETTING DOWN TO BUSINESS—
OPENING THE ACCOUNT

Once you've selected a brokerage to work with, you get started by opening an account with that firm. Personally, I always thought it was pretty self-evident that you have to have an account of some kind to conduct financial affairs. Apparently not everybody thinks so.

I once heard a story about a man who called a brokerage firm and wanted to buy some stock for the first time and he wanted to know how to do it. He was told that he had to open an account and thus fill out forms. The man was stunned; he just wanted to buy stock, not open an account. The broker at the major brokerage wanted to help him, but to become a client it takes opening an account and then the broker buys and sells stock through his account. The man said, "Why should I? I don't have to open an account to buy hamburgers!" But this is a financial firm, and you have to open an account to buy stock. "I don't open an account anywhere!" and the man hung up.

The account is a depository of your cash and whatever assets you hold with your brokerage firm. Every stock that is traded gets registered with the state authorities, each account gets reported to the IRS, and thus the industry is fraught with regulations and paperwork. To make things even trickier, there are many different types of accounts, and you'll have to open the right one. The following is a list of the various account types.

Investment Accounts

An account owned by one person is called an *individual account*. As the name implies, one person is the sole owner of the assets in this account.

An account owned by more than one person is called a *joint account* because the assets are owned jointly. Each person who has an ownership interest in the account is called a *tenant*. One tenant can buy and sell and make deposits or withdrawals without the consent of the other. Following are some ways of handling joint ownership; you'll have to specify which one you want when you fill out the new account form.

- **Joint Tenants with Rights of Survivorship** is an account type that means the two (or more) people who own this account have (almost always) equal ownership in the assets, and when one of them dies the other gets the decedent's interest automatically. This is usually used between a husband and wife.
- **Tenants in Common** means each person owns a certain percentage of the assets (it is an equal percentage unless otherwise

specified), and when one person on the account dies, his or her interest goes to the estate, to be settled according to will.

- **Community Property** only applies to married couples of community property states (Arizona, California, Idaho, Louisiana, New Mexico, Nevada, Texas, Washington, and Wisconsin) where each tenant has an undivided 50 percent interest in all assets acquired during marriage, except for gifts and inheritances. When one spouse dies, half the assets transfer to the estate.

- **Custodial accounts** are set up for minor children under the Uniform Gift to Minors Act (UGMA) or the Uniform Transfer to Minors Act (UTMA). Because one has to be of legal age to make investments (old enough to enter into a contract), assets are held in a custodial account where one adult (the custodian) invests and acts on behalf of one minor. Any assets deposited to or invested within a custodial account are permanently and irrevocably the minor's property. Taxes are reported under the minor's Social Security number, and are taxed at the minor's rate. Children under age 14 can earn up to $1,400 of investment income tax free, and any amount over that is taxed at the parent's rate. After age 14 years, all income is taxed at the minor's rate. Only one adult can serve as the custodian. Once the minor is of legal age (varies from state to state) the account can be converted to a regular individual investment account.

- **Trust accounts** hold the assets that have been set up for a legally created trust. A trust is a separate legal entity, almost like a person or a business. A trust is created for assets or property given by one person (a trustor) for the benefit of another person (a beneficiary), to be managed and watched over by a third person (a trustee) who has the responsibility to follow the trustor's wishes. Those assets have to be held somewhere, and if they are to be invested in stocks, bonds or mutual funds, then they will be held in a trust account.

- **Partnership and corporate accounts** are for established businesses and companies. There is usually a little more paperwork involved, especially when it comes to determining who gets to act on behalf of the partnership or corporation. Investment clubs are technically partnerships, but many firms have a separate investment club account application.

Retirement Accounts

Investment accounts like the types mentioned in the previous section have no special tax benefit. Your brokerage sends you and the IRS a 1099 form every year for your earned interest, dividends, and capital gains. Retirement accounts, though, have some very significant tax benefits, which I'll explain. The only catch is that you can't touch the money without suffering a penalty until you are of retirement age (59½).

Individual Retirement Accounts (IRAs) allow you to deposit up to $4,000 a year starting in 2005. Anyone with earned income (wages, salaries, etc.) can deposit money to an IRA. If you are not covered by any employer-sponsored retirement plan (like a 401(k)), your contribution is tax deductible. If you do have an employer-sponsored plan, your IRA contribution may be fully or partly deductible depending on your income. In all cases you get tax-deferred growth. You can invest your contributions in things like stocks, bonds, and mutual funds, and let the money grow tax deferred, so you don't have to pay taxes on the earnings until after you take the money out, some time after age 59½. You don't pay capital gains taxes on your trades in your IRA (but you can't write off your losses, either). IRA distributions, assuming you take them after age 59½, are taxed as ordinary income.

Only one person can be the owner of an IRA account. The "I" stands for "individual," and there is no such thing as a joint IRA. There is such a thing as a *spousal IRA*, where a working spouse can make retirement contributions for a nonworking spouse.

You can open and fund an IRA as late as April 15 and still get your deduction for the previous year. So you have up until April 15, 2006 to get a 2005 deduction.

Roth IRA accounts were created by the 1997 Taxpayer Relief Act. They allow you to put up to $4,000 into a retirement account a year, but you cannot deduct it from your taxes. However, instead of paying taxes on the growth later, the Roth IRA lets you withdraw what you've put in *plus* what you've earned *tax free*. This is sometimes called a back-end IRA because the real tax benefits come later. A regular or traditional IRA gives you a deduction now and you pay tax later, while a Roth IRA gives you no deduction now but gives you a tax break later. Which is better for you? You should talk to your accountant about it, but generally the younger you are when you start, the greater your nest egg is going to grow by retirement age, therefore the bigger benefit will come from having a Roth IRA. However, the amount you can contribute to a Roth IRA is reduced if your gross income is over $95,000 ($150,000 if married filing jointly) and eliminated if you make more than $110,000 ($160,000 if married filing jointly).

SEP, SARSEP, SIMPLE, and Keogh accounts are retirement plans set up for self-employed people or as a retirement plan for employees of small companies. I won't go into the details or differences here, but like a traditional IRA, they provide a current tax deduction, and offer tax-deferred growth until withdrawn from the account. No new SARSEP plans can be implemented; they have been replaced by SIMPLE plans.

Opening the Account

Now we're ready to get this show started. Once you've selected the type of account you need, the first step in establishing your investment or retirement account is to fill out the *new account application*. In the Internet era, paperwork may not actually involve a piece of paper. Some firms will require your signature on a piece of paper, while others will accept your application by phone or by filling out a form on their Web site with your name, address, Social Security number, etc. Some may allow you to fill out the online form, then mail you the paperwork that has been completed and merely awaits your signature.

Some firms will allow you to open a cash investment account or an IRA or Roth IRA online or over the phone. However, if you want to open an account with a margin trading feature, you will have to sign on the dotted line. Margin accounts have their own rules, and you'll have to sign a margin account application saying that you've read and understand the rules and specifically want to open a margin account.

Minimum Requirement. Just like the sign at the amusement park that says you have to be at least 48 inches tall to ride the roller coaster, you may have to fund the account with a minimum deposit in order to trade with a particular firm. Some firms have relatively high minimums while some have no minimums at all.

Fund the Account.   This part is pretty simple. Brokerage firms are quite accommodating when it comes to taking money. You can deposit a check, money order, or cashier's check. You will not be able to fund the account with cash, either by mail or in person. That's just asking for trouble. Sorry, you will not be able to fund the account by credit card, either. There are certain specific rules that govern borrowing funds to make investments, and using a credit card is one way of borrowing money. Yes, I know we could all build up our frequent flyer miles, but alas, no.

While all brokerage firms will accept a personal check, they may require that the check clear the bank (typically within five business days) before you can invest the money, especially in high-risk securities like penny stocks or options. Money orders and cashier's checks are cleared on deposit. You can also fund the account with a wire transfer from your bank. Wire transfers usually cost a few dollars, but they're bank guaranteed so they are also considered cleared on deposit.

Transferring Accounts.   When people get tired of paying a broker high fees to mishandle their money, they often decide that they would rather mishandle it themselves. However, the really smart ones decide to transfer their account to a new brokerage firm.

To transfer accounts, go to the firm to which you will transfer assets and fill out one of their account transfer forms. Return it along with a photocopy of your last statement of the account you want to transfer.

The Depository Trust Corporation oversees the transfer of investments from one brokerage firm to another. If you do a full account transfer—that is, all the assets of one account move to a different firm—the firms' transfer departments will use an electronic system called Automated Customer Account Transfer (ACAT). ACAT transfers take seven business days to complete, starting from the time the brokerage firm receiving the transfer form acknowledges the transfer.

Power of Attorney.   Let me clear this up: Adding a power of attorney to your account does not mean hiring a lawyer. Sometimes I just say the word "attorney" and people jump. Power of attorney means giving someone else authority to act on your behalf. Someone with a power of attorney can do things for you, such as call your broker, get account information, or place a trade. A stockbroker is only allowed to give specific account information to either the account owner or to someone to whom the owner has granted power of attorney. Very commonly, a husband and wife grant each other power of attorney of their IRAs. Like most things, the account owner fills out a form to grant someone else power of attorney.

There are two levels of authority. *Limited Power of Attorney* gives the person who is granted the power the ability to get account information and place trades on behalf of the account owner. *Full Power of Attorney* allows the grantee to withdraw money from the account as well, and is usually granted because the account owner is incapacitated in some way. A full power of attorney is more restrictive and harder to get than the limited variety, so ask your brokerage firm's representative what it takes to get one, or if you really even need one.

Breadth of Products

When we think of trading, we think of buying and selling stocks. But there's a whole lot more to the financial world than stocks, and there could very well be something in it for you. Bonds, mutual funds, options, limited partnerships, commodities, and futures are financial instruments that you can invest in. Each has its own characteristics, risks, and opportunities.

It all depends what you want to do, of course. Plenty of people are only interested in trading shares of stock. That's fine. Some people may want to consolidate all their financial activity under one roof, even under one account. Anyone interested in options trading and complex strategies will want to use a brokerage that can accommodate their needs. If you want the broadest array of financial products, or think you might use them one day, look for an online brokerage firm that offers as much as possible.

Following is a list of some of the products offered by many online firms, along with some questions you might ask of a prospective brokerage. Don't worry if you're not sure what these things are. They will be covered in more detail in later chapters.

- Stocks represent equity ownership in a company. When you own a share of stock, you own a piece (maybe one hundred-millionth) of the company. That's why stocks and things that impart ownership are called *equity securities*. All the online brokerages handle stocks, of course, or they'd be pretty much useless.

- Find out if the brokerage offers dividend reinvestment programs. This allows you take the dividend that you'd normally get in cash and use it to buy additional fractional shares of stock. Now, fractional shares don't really exist, they're just a bookkeeping entry. Still, half of a $50 stock is worth $25, and if you liquidate your position you will get cash for the fraction of a share. See if there is a fee for this service (it might be something like 5 percent).
- Not all stocks are the same. There are certain stocks that trade in a market called the *Bulletin Board* or the *Pink Sheets*. Again, I'll cover these in more detail in Chapter 11, but these markets are for thinly traded stocks that don't qualify to be listed on a major exchange. Not all brokers will trade these stocks, and some won't do it online but will want you to phone in your orders.
- The world is your oyster, and you may also find opportunities in foreign markets. For those brokerages that offer access to foreign stocks, inquire whether they trade on the foreign exchanges directly, or do so through a market maker. A market maker may take a cut for his trouble and you may not get as favorable an execution.

Account and Trading Practices

Every firm has its own policies, and if you are seriously looking at doing business with them, you'll need to know their policies ahead of time. Don't make assumptions. Find the answers by going to their Web sites and asking customer service reps. Read the paperwork that they give you. Have a pen and paper ready and ask questions because, once again, knowledge is power and the more you know, the more comfortable you will be going forward. The following are some suggested questions to ask the broker:

- How are uninvested funds handled? Here you're asking how your cash balances are put to work for you. Will it earn interest, or will the money be swept into a money market fund? A money market fund is a special type of mutual fund that invests only in certain things, such as short-term bonds and CDs, and is managed to maintain $1 a share. They work like cash, and are called *cash equivalents*. You may need a minimum deposit to open a money fund feature (perhaps $1,000) and keep a certain minimum to maintain it (maybe $100), otherwise your deposits don't earn anything. Also find out how often they sweep cash into the money fund, whether daily or weekly (more often is better). If you have a fairly large deposit that you don't plan to invest at the moment, ask if they offer a higher-yielding money fund with a high minimum. Do they offer government, treasury, or tax-exempt money funds? How do their rates compare? Deep discount online brokers charge low commissions but may offer lower money market yields.

- Does your brokerage have a cash-up-front requirement on new orders? If so, that means you will have to have the money in the account at the time of the order, or else they will not allow the trade to go through. Even though the Federal Reserve allows you to pay for your stocks up to three business days after you buy them (known as T+3, where T stands for Trade Date), your broker is allowed to insist that you have the money on deposit ahead of time. If your broker requires cash up front, there are a few considerations you will have to understand.

1. When you place a new buy order, you must have sufficient cash or margin cash available to cover the minimum required deposit (see the chapter on margin trading). If there are not enough funds to cover the purchase, the firm will reject and cancel the order.
2. There has to be enough money or cash available to cover all your new open buy orders as they come in. Each new buy order will be evaluated as to whether there is enough money to cover the new order *and* all existing open buy orders. So if you send three buy orders, and there is enough money to cover the first two but not all three, the third order will be rejected.
3. It's called a "cash-up-front" requirement or buy order, but it is also a "shares-up-front" requirement on your sell orders. You must have the shares on deposit in your account before your brokerage will accept a sell order. Without that restric-

tion, you would be able to sell the shares and then deliver the stock certificate within three business days.

Why do some firms have this restriction? Usually the deep discount firms have a cash-up-front requirement because they have to work on very slim profit margins. It's inefficient and expensive to chase after people who are late on making deposits.

- Does your broker accept stop orders on all securities? A stop order is usually used to sell your stock if it falls down to a certain price (sometimes called a stop loss order). Strictly speaking, the stock exchanges handle stop orders, but the over-the-counter markets do not. However, your brokerage or its affiliate market maker may still accept those orders. Not all will accept stop orders on Nasdaq or OTCBB stocks. Not all will accept stop orders on exchange listed stocks. You have to ask.
- Individual investors now have the ability to trade while the stock exchanges are closed. For many years, institutional investors were able to trade outside standard market hours (9:30 A.M. to 4:00 P.M., Eastern Time), sometimes taking advantage of news releases that came out after the close. Now, you and I have the ability to trade in *extended market hours* after the market is closed and before it opens. Computer systems called Electronic Communication Networks (or ECNs) match your buy and sell orders with someone else that placed orders in that system. There are multiple ECNs. Usually, your online brokerage will offer access to at least one of them, and some have access to more than one (it's a good thing if they do).

Margin Policies

For those of you who trade on margin, or think you may, you'll want to pay very close attention to your brokerage firm's margin policies.

Every brokerage firm must adhere to certain minimum requirements as to how much they can lend you against the value of your portfolio. However, a firm is allowed to implement policies that are stricter than the requirements mandated by federal and stock exchange rules. The rules specify how much equity you have to have to start with, what percent of the value of your portfolio you can borrow, and how far your account can fall in value before you'll have to deposit more money or sell off shares.

For example, the federal regulation says you must maintain $2,000 in equity before you can borrow anything against it. Charles Schwab requires that you maintain at least $5,000 equity. That means, if you want to buy $3,000 in stock, the feds say you have to put up $2,000, but Schwab says you have to put up all $3,000 (assuming you have no other assets in your account).

Ask a prospective brokerage firm what their minimum margin account maintenance policy is. Regulations say an account must maintain 25 percent equity, but it's very common for an individual firm to require a minimum of 30 to 35 percent equity. Many firms will not lend anything against stocks trading under $5 a share, and many will limit the amount they will lend against what they consider highly volatile stocks.

There is also the matter of how much interest you'll pay if you borrow on margin. Margin interest rates are based on a figure published in the *Wall Street Journal* called the *broker call rate*, and each firm tacks a percentage onto that rate and passes the markup along to you. The added percentage varies among firms and the rate is often tiered so you pay a lower rate if you borrow more money.

Trading and Account Fees

Online trading has brought about super low commissions. One consequence of such deep discount trading fees, however, is that additional services that once were free may now cost a little something extra. I don't care much for surprises, especially when they cost money, so make sure you are made aware of any additional costs ahead of time.

You can place orders by different mechanisms, but there may be a different fee depending what channel you use. Ameritrade, for example, used to charge one fee for an order placed on the Internet, a higher fee if it was placed by touch-tone phone, and the highest fee for a broker-assisted market order. Also, the fee may be different based on the type of order. Ameritrade charges an extra $5 for broker-assisted limit orders. Some firms charge annual or quarterly account maintenance fees, but they will waive the fees if you keep a minimum balance or do a minimum amount of trading. Ask if there are fees for certain extra services. There may be charges for more time or labor-intensive services including:

- Ordering out stock certificates
- Picking up checks from a branch office
- Real time quotes
- Mandatory or involuntary reorganizations
- Holding nonstandard assets, such as limited partnerships
- Exit fees for transferring out your account

Resources and High-End Services

Research services should not be overlooked. I give higher marks to those firms that offer proprietary or premium third-party research to their customers with no extra fee. Also look for tax planning, retirement planning, and asset allocation tools. Some of the low cost firms, like Brown, don't really offer research, just links to sites like zachs.com (which is information you can get on your own).

Are you a high roller? See if you qualify for the high roller treatment. There's a saying in business that 20 percent of your customers are 80 percent of your business, and that's certainly true for the online brokerage industry. Many firms compete for the very active and wealthy investors by offering premium services. E*Trade offers Power E*Trade, Schwab offers Signature Services, and Harris Direct offers Select Client Services. You have to do a certain amount of trading or have a certain amount on deposit with the firm in order to qualify for high-end services.

Open Financial Data

Do you really want to save some time? Users of Quicken, MS Money (or later versions), or the Microsoft Investor Web site may want to consider using a broker that supports Open Financial Exchange, or OFX for short. OFX is a standard by which you can download your account activity directly into any one of these three programs. Quicken and Money are personal finance programs produced by Intuit and Microsoft, respectively. Microsoft Investor is a free online service that provides many of the same features. OFX allows you to securely download your account activity directly into your computer, which saves you a lot of time by not having to enter transactions manually. OFX uses dedicated SSL-enabled servers, so your account information is always encrypted.

All in all, there is no one brokerage firm that can be all things to all people. Many people have accounts at several firms, each for their own reasons. I once read about a man who had an account with Schwab because he had over a million dollars with them and got very good executions on large positions. He also had an account with Ameritrade for its very low commissions, and he had an account with Datek when he wanted rapid-fire execution. I think it comes down to priorities. If you're clear about what you want in a brokerage firm and what's most important to you, your decisions will be easier.

STOCKS AND INVESTING

My American dream includes taking care of myself by not working for someone else. My American dream includes starting and owning my own company. I did not have to do it that way. How would you like to own a major corporation? Chances are you already do, or at least a piece of one if you own a share of stock. That piece of a corporation is a stock, or a share. If you have purchased stock +in a company, you and the other stockholders in that company are the owners.

But owning stock isn't *really* like being Donald Trump. While owning stocks does make you a part owner in the company, it does not mean that you will have to go over the latest sales figures or plan a new advertising budget. The beauty of owning stocks is that collectively, stockholders do own a large piece of publicly traded companies and have a big say in how a company operates. When you are a stockowner you are entitled to share in the corporation's assets and profits. Although short-term it might feel like you own a piece of electronic paper or a data entry in a ledger book, longer-term you are a profit-sharing owner of a piece of the company.

For most investors, the reason for buying stock isn't to own a company, it is actually much simpler—it is to make money! Pretty darn simple but true all the same. When you buy a stock, you make an investment bet that the company's stock will increase in value. Therein lies the mystery of stocks: They have no intrinsic value, but the stock market assigns them one based on what you and other investors are willing to pay. In fact, day to day the value might change for no discernable reason. But you have to know that over the long haul, stocks on average have been profitable. Again please remember that stocks go up, on average, 7 out of 10 years and to be honest, I can't find better odds than that if I tried.

Why buy a stock? Simply because you think it's going to go up. You are buying into the vision of the company. You are becoming an owner. Why sell a stock? Because you think it's going to go down. Don't try to outthink this process. You don't buy a stock to own a piece of the American Dream or to have a souvenir or a right to the earnings of the company. You don't get any of those things. You don't even get a piece of paper anymore. You get a journal entry.

How do you know what stocks are good? Some would say, "You have a good stock if the fundamentals are sound at the company," or "Good stocks are the stocks of companies that make a lot of money." It is comical that no one can actually define what is a good stock versus what is a piece of junk…if only it were so easy! Sure, sometimes there is an intersection between stock performance and company management, but more often than not, how a stock does is a function of many different variables—everything from the economy and interest rates to the sector that the company is in, to the company's earnings. A good analogy is horseracing. The company is the horse, but the outcome is also affected by the jockey, the conditions on the field, and the weather. In sports, we know that many people bet on teams to win, but the best team doesn't always win. It is the same with the stock market. The company is only part of the equation, which is really an important concept because you won't always be right even when you pick the best companies.

WHAT IS THE STOCK MARKET?

When people refer to the stock market, they are simply refer-
ring to a public place where buyers and sellers make transactions, directly or via intermediaries. The two main types of
stock markets are exchanges and electronic markets.

Exchanges, such as the New York Stock Exchange (NYSE) and
the American Stock Exchange (Amex), are physical locations
where stock transactions are conducted auction style—meaning
traders try to negotiate with each other to find the best price. On
the NYSE (also known as the Big Board), firms give their buy and
sell orders to their floor brokers. On any given day, more than a billion shares may change hands on the NYSE, which has been around
since 1789 and lists more than 3,000 companies' stocks.

The National Association of Securities Dealers Automated Quo-
tation System (more commonly known as Nasdaq) is the world's
first electronic market, enabling brokers to conduct trades from
around the country via telephones and computers. On the Nasdaq,
instead of specialists matchmaking the trading, market makers—
dealers who specialize in a specific stock—compete with each other
over the electronic system to buy and sell a stock. The Nasdaq,
which was born in 1971 and lists more than 5,000 stocks, tends to
be more active than the NYSE, and often trades more than two billion shares in one session.

To be listed on the Nasdaq, NYSE, or Amex, companies must
meet certain requirements regarding market value, assets, or earnings. While they vary, in general, the NYSE's requirements are
the toughest, which means the NYSE tends to have older, more-
established companies. The Nasdaq includes a range of companies,
big (such as Microsoft) and small, but it is generally known as a market for emerging companies, with a bent toward technology firms.

The Stock Exchanges

How do the markets work? A lot of times it feels like a video game
if you jump online and buy and sell stocks. You point at something
with your mouse, click on it, and something happens almost imme-

diately. It's wonderful to have these almost instantaneous executions, and I think it's been great for investors and traders. Not that long ago, people had to call a broker who would write their order on a ticket that got carried on a conveyor belt to someone at a trading desk. This great benefit also comes with a potential hazard—the "click and it's done" power of the Internet make trading so easy that it's quite possible to forget, or not even know, how it got done to begin with.

In fact, there is a lot more going on than meets the eye, and a lot happens that you can't see when you're sitting in front of your computer. As much as it seems like it, you do not have direct access to the markets. Your brokerage has methods of handling your order and getting it to the exchanges. Each stock exchange—the New York, American, Nasdaq, and others—has rules and procedures that determine how your orders get executed. Your order may have to compete with dozens or hundreds of other orders coming in at nearly the same time. While you can't see the order desks, or the trading pits, they are there nonetheless.

It's easy to enter orders, and it's just as easy to get the results of the order. This chapter is all about what happens in between. People called me all the time saying, "I saw the stock trade at my price but my order didn't get filled!" There's a reason for that, and it becomes clear when you understand how the stock markets work. I believe that it's just as important that you know how your orders get fulfilled as it is that you know how to enter the order. The New York Stock Exchange and the Nasdaq operate differently, and I can't tell you the number of people who've thought they worked the same way only to get very frustrated when they found out otherwise.

By the way, sometimes the exchanges do get it wrong, and don't fill orders that were due to be fulfilled or they execute them poorly. It happens. When you know how the exchanges work, you'll also know if you should have gotten a better deal.

Let's find out what happens after you click the "send order" button.

The Auction Markets

A stock exchange is a private organization where its members meet in a single place to buy and sell shares of ownership in a corpora-

tion whose shares are listed on that exchange. You've seen the
building at the corner of Wall Street and Broad Street in lower
Manhattan that houses the New York Stock Exchange. It's about the
size of a football field. If you ever get the chance, you can take the
tour of the observation gallery and get a view of the trading floor
from three stories up. It's free, you just need to arrive ahead of time
to get a ticket then come back later to take the tour.

Since the exchange is a private organization, anyone who wants
access to the exchange *floor* (where the trading activity takes place)
has to be a member. To be a member, an individual or corporation
must purchase a membership, or a *seat* on the exchange. There are
only 1,366 seats on the New York Stock Exchange, they can only
be bought from someone who already owns one and they sell for
over $2 million a piece. Now it does seem somewhat ironic that a
membership is called a "seat" because there are no chairs on the
exchange floor. (Actually, once upon a time the exchange traded
stocks one company at a time, and members did sit in chairs while
waiting for their stock to be called out.)

So who are the members of the stock exchanges? They fall
largely into three categories:

- Brokers who execute trades on their clients' behalf. These clients may be institutions like mutual funds or pension accounts,
  or they may be retail clients of a brokerage firm.
- So-called "two-dollar" brokers who assist other brokers when
  they get very busy (a long time ago, they got paid $2 a trade for
  helping out).
- Traders who act for their own accounts using their own capital.

The Auction Process

The stock exchange is a huge auction. There are a number of people who want to buy at the lowest price possible, and there are a
number of people who want to sell for the highest price they can
get. Buyers and sellers (represented by their brokerage firm's *floor
brokers*) compete against one another, each stating their prices by
verbal outcry (shouting). At any time, there is at least one buyer
willing to pay more than anyone else and will outbid all the other
prospective buyers, effectively raising the bid price on the stock. On
the other side of the deal, there must be at least one seller who

really wants to cash out and will undercut the price of any other seller, effectively lowering the asking price on the stock. You've got one person who says, "I'll buy for this" and someone else who says, "I'll sell for that." A trade takes place when a buyer and a seller agree on a price. Once a transaction is done, it is reported to the exchange and is disseminated over the *consolidated tape* normally within 90 seconds. Of course the one-inch wide strip of paper streaming from a bell jar telegraph is long obsolete, but the electronic systems that report each trade are still referred to as the tape. When a trade is done, the auction process starts over.

It sounds cliché to say stock prices fluctuate along with supply and demand, but when you have a chance to see how the market works and how prices change moment by moment, you can see that it's really true. There are always a certain number of buyers willing to pay for the stock (that's the demand), and a number of sellers who want to get money for their shares (that's the supply). Let's say company XYZ just announced that they've landed a big contract. So the auction process begins. The buyers for XYZ start lining up, each saying what they're willing to pay for shares, and of course some are willing to pay more than others. Ultimately one buyer will outbid all the others and let's say the most anyone will pay is $26.25. At the same time, there are people who want to sell XYZ, and they line up each offering shares for sale. One seller is going to undercut all the other sellers, and let's say that someone is willing to let his shares go for $26.38. Right at this moment, XYZ is bid at $26.25 and offered at $26.38.

Now some new buyers come into the marketplace, and they really want to own XYZ shares, so they are willing to meet the offer made by the lowest seller. A buyer and a seller agree on a price, and a trade gets done and reported at $26.38. If the aggressive buying continues, then eventually the buyers will have snapped up all the shares that were offered for sale at $26.38 until there is no one left who is willing to sell that low. If a buyer still wants to buy, he will have to meet the price of the next lowest offer, which may be $26.50. If people are still buying, all the shares offered for sale at $26.50 get bought up, then all the shares offered at $26.75, then the shares offered at $27, and so on.

There is a limited quantity of shares wanted to buy or offered for sale at any given price level. When that supply is exhausted, the price moves to the next price level until that supply is exhausted as well, and then the price trend continues as long as the demand is unabated.

Meanwhile, the person who was the top bidder at $26.25 sees that he is now rapidly being outbid. If he wants to buy XYZ, he's going to have to raise his bid. He may increase his bid to $26.50 then $26.75, or whatever he has to do to chase that particular stock. Prospective sellers, on the other hand, also know that XYZ Corp. hit the big time, and they may start retracting their low offers because they think they can get more for their shares. What happens is that the demand grows at higher prices while the supply contracts. That's what pushes prices up.

The same thing happens in the other direction. Let's say XYZ has spiked to $32. By this time the feeding frenzy may have subsided as the first round of buyers who clamored to get shares at any price have bought their shares and have left the auction. Now prospective buyers may start to think that $32 is a little expensive and stop entering new buy orders. At the same time, some XYZ owners may start to think that $32 looks like a pretty decent opportunity to take a profit. Now the auction process continues, but this time sellers start putting in more orders to sell at $32 and increase the supply of shares at that price level. Buyers are becoming more reluctant, so maybe the highest bid is now $31.75. One seller may decide that this is as good as it's going to get and so he decides to meet the buyer's price. A trade is completed and reported at $31.75. As more aggressive sellers come into the marketplace, undercutting all other sellers, they will eventually exhaust the demand for shares at $31.75. Now anyone who wants to sell will have to meet the price of the next highest bidder at $31.63, then $31.50, then $31.25, then $31, and so on. A falling stock price can also be considered an increasing demand for cash.

Research Analysts

Research analysts are a touchy topic. When it comes to stocks, everybody has an opinion. The folks who get paid for their opinions are analysts. They can be your best friend or they can be your worst enemy. Analysts' opinions are often based on the research they do and who they do it for. The analyst community has been picked on (rightfully) as there is no real benchmark or tool for rating an individual analyst's performance. Just understand that an analyst does not work for you and thus you must take their advice with a grain salt. This does not mean you should ignore them. In fact, pay attention, but do realize they are not your Buddha on the mountain.

An analyst follows the performance of a group of companies, often by industry, and makes recommendations whether these companies would make good investments. They gather all sorts of information about particular stocks—from basic financial data to arcane tidbits about the competition—and analyze all these factors to come up with investment advice.

Three major parts of an analyst's job are:

1. Assigning ratings to stocks, such as strong buy, hold, and sell;
2. Putting a price target on a stock for a given period. Usually the period is 12 months, so as to adjust for temporary swings in the market; and
3. Making earnings estimates for companies.

Positive or negative ratings, price targets, or earnings out-looks from analysts, especially the highly regarded ones, often move stock prices.

Stock analysts are divided into two groups: the buy side and the sell side. Buy-side analysts work for mutual funds, private money managers, and hedge funds—in other words, the buyers—and tell their bosses which stocks to buy. Sell-side analysts, who work for the investment banks that sell the securities, pass along their advice to individual and institutional investors.

Today, it's difficult to pinpoint exactly what the function of a Wall Street analyst is. Analysts still perform research, and they still make recommendations. But analysts can have many masters, with diverging interests. Research must help the brokerage's sales force generate orders. It must also guide institutional clients (big mutual fund companies like Fidelity or Putnam). And as we saw with corruption on Wall Street, increasingly, analysts play a vital role in helping their firms drum up underwriting and mergers-and-acquisitions advisory business. Somewhere in all of this is the interest of the individual investor seeking unbiased investment advice.

Research is simply background material to help you understand what's going on in a particular sector of the market. It is not, however, a reliable way to pick stocks.

The Food Chain of Stock Information:
What's Your Position?

In the past, the more money you had, the better the information you seemed to get. That was the way of Wall Street. When you hear news about a stock, stop and think for a moment. Who has heard this news before you? One of the pet peeves many investors have is in dealing with a company's disclosure of information, particularly when the news is bad. The individual investor can feel like chopped liver when they find out a stock that they bought is down 50 percent or more on bad news. I assure you that even today the individual is treated like chopped liver when it comes to news that you can use. Too many other eyeballs will see it before you do, so be cautious.

Keep in mind that news on the East Coast can hit while investors are sleeping on the West Coast and even before you have your Wheaties, your stock can be down 15 percent in a "West Coast Dump." I have even seen bad news hit a stock while the CEO was talking in an airplane. News moves fast and your sources might be less than informed so pick companies that you can trust and believe in.

When you buy a company that has 30 analysts covering the stock, you must prepare yourself for short-term periods of great annoyance, as they jockey to make minute changes in their opinions that mean very little in the long run. If 30 analysts have buys, and part of their pay is dependent on generating ideas that create trading commissions for their employer, there is only one direction they can go, and vice versa.

Does this mean you should just cast your lot with professional portfolio managers who have tons of influence? Not at all. Don't forget that you can call companies yourself directly for information. Call during off peak times (the day of the earnings release when the stock is down six points is not one of them), and have ten questions in hand about the company that aren't available on the second page of the annual report. Most Investor Relations departments are happy to spend 15 minutes with you.

And that is 15 minutes well spent. Why? Because at the end of the day, you need to think for yourself. Your money is of little concern to anyone other than you.

Wall Street Research Is Better

Controversy over stock research still rages on Wall Street, years after New York Attorney General Eliot Spitzer's investigation into conflicts of interest between analysts and investment bankers triggered dramatic reforms in the way research is conducted.

A whole new set of rules now governs how analysts communicate both with the companies they follow and the investment bankers at their own firms. Two pages of disclosures are included at the back of every research report, showing how the stock has performed after an opinion changes and how ratings for investment-banking clients differ from other stocks covered by that firm. Analysts' pay is now tied more to performance and less to investment-banking deals, and it has declined significantly as a result.

The reforms have been costly for firms, and behind closed doors they are roundly ridiculed. Change will continue to shape this new era of Wall Street research. For example, firms now have to hand out reports from independent outfits along with their own in-house research—a major provision of their $1.4 billion April, 2003 settlement with Spitzer and other securities regulators.

Already, one thing that should silence some of that closed-door sniping is clear: Wall Street research is getting better. Since the Enron and Worldcom debacle, research has become more objective, more original, and more accurate. There is less regurgitated-type scribe work. Firms are doing their own proprietary research. There is more actual analysis going on.

Data from StarMine, an independent research firm that tracks analysts' stock-picking and earnings forecasting, make the case. Throughout the 1990s and until 2001, only 1 percent of stocks were rated sell. By 2003, 14 percent of stocks rated by the ten biggest Wall Street firms carry the lowest rating, according to StarMine.

Furthermore, StarMine calculates that in 2002, following analysts' advice would have had a slightly negative impact on portfolios on average. But in 2003, it would have added 2.2 percentage points to returns. Not bad. To be fair, in 2004, StarMine found that analysts' advice would have had no calculable impact on returns.

The most important change for the better is in the quality of analysis. In the bad old days, research on the same company from different firms was often barely distinguishable. Now, written commentary in stock reports is more independent, more thought-

provoking, and better represents the upside and downside potential for a stock than the bubble era's much-hyped reports. Analyst
reports are also more diverse, reflecting more originality in analysis
and research tools.

The biggest complaint on research now is that it still reflects
short-term thinking—focusing too much on the next quarter's
results—rather than the two- to five-year time horizon most investors would like to see. Analysts get caught up in short-term issues
that aren't fundamental to the long-term growth of the business.

So, even though Wall Street research is better, is it good
enough? The reforms are still just getting under way. But a few years
into the process, with lots of modifications already in place, the
result so far is a welcome change for the better.

BUYING STOCKS ON MARGIN

You can buy a whole house without a single dollar outlaid. In fact,
you can buy just about anything without paying the entire amount
up front. Stocks are no different, thanks to buying on margin. A
popular definition of margin is using money borrowed from a
broker/dealer to purchase securities. You are leveraging your position in stocks and paying interest for the right to do so.

When you buy a stock on margin, you pay for a portion and leverage, or borrow, the rest (up to 50 percent on an initial investment)
from your broker. The upshot on leveraging is if the stock goes up,
you make a far greater profit on your initial investment. As with everything else, there is a catch. This works both ways, so if the stock goes
down, you may end up owing more than your upfront investment.

Here's how it works: Let's say you want to buy 100 shares in
XYZ's stock at $100 per share. When you buy on margin, you pay
$5,000 and your broker lends you the other $5,000. XYZ's stock
rises 50 percent to $150, putting your total investment at $15,000,
and you decide to sell. You pay your broker the $5,000 you owe, and
you keep the other $10,000.

What if the stock falls 50 percent? This is the big risk of buying
on margin, in the form of a margin call. If the value of your investment falls below 75 percent of its original value, your broker will
issue a margin call, meaning you have to put more money into your
margin account. If you can't put more money in, you have to sell
the stock and pay the broker back the $5,000. If the stock were to

fall 50 percent from $100 to $50, your investment would be worth only $5,000. That money goes to the broker (plus commissions and interest you owe), and your initial $5,000 is gone.

Even if you decide not to use leverage to buy stocks, margin buying affects all investors because of its impact on the market. During the spring 2000 market swoon, the fact that investors were selling to meet margin calls was cited as a key factor that added to the downward pressure on stocks. For the record, I got murdered in the spring of 2000 and it was not until the summer and fall that I sold out of my technology positions. We all make mistakes but the trick is to sell before the pressure gets to you and the mistakes get compounded.

Here is what you really need to know about margin debt: Understand that excessive margin is a red flag that has historically caused grave, but quick, sell-offs in the market. So when you see margin debt grow on Wall Street, it is usually a sign of excessive speculation. Remember that margin debt is usually in the hands of individuals and not used by firms that routinely handle wealthy institutions and individuals.

INITIAL PUBLIC OFFERINGS (IPOS)

IPOs are when a company first issues stock to the public. IPOs are a bit like a corporate version of a coming-out party. (Let's face it: In the late 1990s IPOs became addictive and compelling.) Depending on the company's prospects for growth, there may be many suitors eager to take part in the bash.

In the dot.com years (1996 through 2000), the IPO market was booming with dot.com offerings as investors big and small scrambled to get a piece of the latest hot technology company coming to market. That led to huge pops, or price increases, on the first day that a stock would trade, but at times it has also led to severe retrenchments in a stock price in the days and weeks following the IPO. So let the buyer beware: Fortunes can be gained and lost fairly quickly in the world of IPOs. Ultimately, IPOs seem to reflect popular opinion and thus Wall Street seems to bring out companies that they think the public wants at that particular point in time. The dot.com IPO boom was followed by companies going public with strong earnings, which was the followed by a big Biotech IPO phase as investors wanted the company that would take advantage of one of the hottest technologies, DNA sequencing.

IPOs may come from established companies that have, for one reason or another, long been closely held by a few large investors. Goldman Sachs, which went public in the spring of 1999, is such an example. Initial offerings may also come from an operation within a larger company, with the parent company eager to open the division to the markets and unlock its shareholder value. An example of this is when AT&T Wireless Group, a division of AT&T, began trading in the spring of 2000.

Most often, IPOs are from relatively new companies looking to tap the public market to fund their expansion plans. Typically, a company begins as a start-up with venture capital funding—private-sector money from well-heeled firms or individuals who make it their business to invest in early-stage companies.

Straight Talk on IPOs

IPOs have long been a hot but volatile facet of the market, and that's especially true now that smaller investors have been getting into the IPO game. Before you rush into an IPO only to find that you bought at the top, you need to know that 85 percent of all IPOs underperform the S&P 500 in their first year (see Figures 9.1 through 9.3).

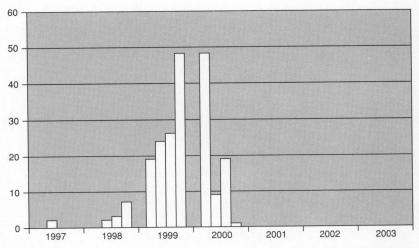

FIGURE 9.1 Number of IPOs Doubling in Price on the First Day of Trading by Quarter, 1997–2003

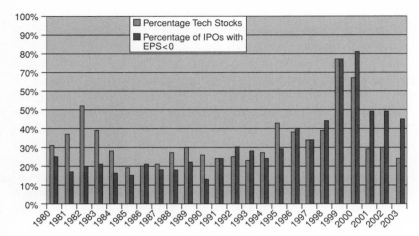

FIGURE 9.2 Fraction of IPOs with Negative Earnings and Fraction of Tech Stocks, 1980–2003

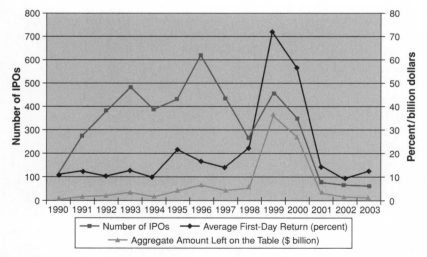

FIGURE 9.3 Average First-Day Return and Aggregate Amount Left on the Table, 1990–2003

INTERNATIONAL STOCKS

Do you have a yen for Japanese stocks? Think German stocks will hit the mark? Okay, the puns are bad, especially since many European nations have changed their currencies to the Euro, but you get the point. Foreign stocks can be a great way to diversify your portfolio and find new opportunities. Buying them has never been easier. But, there are important factors regarding risks and rewards that you should consider when investing overseas. The first is currency.

An investor's return on a stock from a foreign country is tied to changes in currency values between the U.S. dollar and that country's currency. In short, if an investor buys a French stock, and the Euro (the French currency) rises against the dollar between the time you buy and sell the stock, your return is worth more. If the Euro weakens, the return weakens as well.

Beyond the perils and promise of the Euro, there are other matters to consider when investing overseas. Just like homegrown investing, you must find out as much as you can about the company before giving them your money. Investing globally brings a whole new slew of challenges. Some international exchanges don't require companies to disclose as much financial information as U.S. exchanges do, which may result in unforeseeable problems down the road. Also, rules governing trading, taxes, and corporate accounting vary from country to country, and some are much less stringent than others. Moreover, stocks in some emerging countries with less stable governments and economies are vulnerable to sudden leadership changes, surging inflation, and currency problems.

The notion of international stocks offering diversity doesn't always hold true: Often, because many foreign countries rely in part on the U.S. economy for imports and exports, foreign stock markets are vulnerable to U.S. market gyrations.

This isn't to suggest that overseas investing is all gloom and doom. On the contrary, some of the hottest growth areas in the past few years have been beyond U.S. borders. Before you write off emerging markets, remember that the United States itself once fit this very same description.

Investors can tap into foreign countries and foreign markets in a variety of ways. First, many established international companies list stock on U.S. exchanges, either directly or sold as American depository receipts (ADRs). Also, many multinational brokers offer clients the ability to buy stocks on foreign exchanges. Lastly, scores of mutual funds have international offerings focusing on region, country, and even sector specialties within regions. Brokerage groups such as Citigroup and Goldman Sachs are good resources for international market information.

More on Investing Abroad

While the U.S. economic boom and the bull market had a glorious run in the 1990s, like all good things, it did come to an end. During that time period, because of the huge success at home, Americans were reluctant to invest their money abroad. We were continually bombarded with headlines about the Asian economic crisis (Asian flu) and Russia's collapsing economy. Japan struggled out of its worst postwar recession ever, only to fall smack into a new one and Germany's economy stagnated. The fact is that even when some of the world's stock markets do very well, by either absolute or relative measures, they rarely stir the imagination the way visions of Nasdaq can.

Given that many big U.S. blue chips, such as Coca-Cola and International Business Machines (IBM), now derive significant revenue streams from overseas markets, some observers suggest you can keep all your money at home and still have exposure to foreign markets. Investing luminary John Bogle, founder of the Vanguard Group, has argued that placing money abroad is no longer necessary for ensuring a well-diversified portfolio. U.S. equities, which constitute about half of the world's market capitalization, seem indomitable. The benefits of investing abroad appear outweighed by the risks of missing the party at home.

And yet, that perception is wrong.

Diversifying overseas works because even though big global markets may often move in the same direction, they rarely move with the same magnitude. Sure, when the S&P 500 is up, Japan's Nikkei and Germany's Dax are probably going to rise—but not by the same degree. Baltimore-based mutual fund company T. Rowe Price says that over the last ten years, market movements have been correlated roughly half the time. The rest of the time gives one part of a portfolio—the domestic or the foreign—an opportunity to outperform the other.

What will performance in your portfolio be when the rest of the world finally starts leading rather than following the United States? What will performance be if—and this is a big if— the U.S. economy is finally corralled?

The reality of investing is that you don't always have all your money in the right thing. But you don't have all your money in the wrong thing either. If you're in it for the long run, it's probably better to be hedged with some international exposure.

Some Rules for Investing Abroad

The risks and rewards of international investing can be explained in a nutshell. One year you can experience fantastic returns, and miserable returns in the next. And sometimes there won't be a significant change in the fundamentals to explain the difference. After all, most of the economies in Asia look pretty strong right now. But a few years back, the region was rebounding from the post-financial crisis bottom. That doesn't mean you should try to time international markets. You need to make them a vital part of your portfolio to help diversify risk and take advantage of overseas opportunities.

What is a good strategy for investing overseas? Some financial planners prefer a sector strategy over a regional one. In other words, invest in broad-based international general equity funds, supplemented with companies listing here or sector-specific international funds, such as technology or biotech.

Another financial planner might have more problems with being in a China fund, so he'll prefer a more straightforward approach. He might find that the best way to buy international equities is through a broad-based mutual fund.

The real question of strategy is why not Latin America? Europe? In general, it seems the more diversification the better when it comes to international investing. That would include broad-based funds, regional funds, country-specific funds, and an individual stock or two. You never know where the next hot market will be— or the next frigid one.

One final tip for investing abroad. One day a prospective international investor asked me if he should be investing in Russian Telecom. He said it looked "hot" and "a friend" told him it was a good move.

After a moment of thought, I asked a very important question. "How many digits are in a Russian phone number?"

The man was puzzled. "I dunno. What does that have to do with anything?"

I explained. "If you don't know anything about the Russian phone business, then why are you investing in it?"

Whether the company is located in Paris, France or Paris, Texas, know the business before buying the stock. Don't use proximity as an excuse to avoid the homework! Otherwise you might be out of your league.

INVESTING 101: GROWTH VERSUS VALUE

Growth stocks are generally those with above-average earnings growth, price-earnings ratios, and market-book ratios. Value stocks are lower in each case but offer above-average yields. Legendary investor John Bogle examined 60 years of growth funds (mutual funds with stated growth objectives and a record of above-average volatility) and value funds (seeking both growth and income, and demonstrating average to below-average volatility).

His study was interesting. In the early years, growth funds were in control and clearly the winners over value funds. Value stocks then enjoyed a huge resurgence and thus made up almost the entire earlier deficit. Then, growth stocks outperformed and then value stocks started to dominate again.

When all of these cyclical fluctuations for the full six decades were put together, the investment in value stocks was equal to about nine-tenths of the investment in growth stocks. For the last 60 years, the compound total returns were: growth, 11.7 percent; value, 11.5 percent—a tiny difference. That constitutes a draw in anyone's book and is a classic example of why you don't want to try to outsmart the markets.

DO STOCK SPLITS REALLY MATTER?

Would you rather have six of one, or a half dozen of the other? They're the same thing, right? But in the investing world, stock splits work a little differently in the minds of investors.

When a company's stock price gets very high, some investors may shy away from purchasing it. In an effort to lure investors with a lower price tag, companies often split their stock in two or more equal parts. For example, if XYZ Co.'s stock climbs to $120, the company may announce a 2-for-1 stock split, meaning shareholders would get two $60 shares for every $120 share they hold. The underlying value remains the same. (Companies can also perform reverse stock splits— splitting a stock 1-to-5, for example—in order to raise the stock price.)

If nothing has really changed, why are stock splits such a hot topic? Because investor sentiment may think that a cheaper stock is more attractive and thus different. Some investors like to purchase shares in 50-share or 100-share lots, and a big price tag for one stock may keep them away.

Many investors monitor stock-split announcements and buy shares on an announcement, hoping to see a pop in the price once the split takes effect.

Point/Counterpoint on Stock Splits

As is the case with just about every element of the stock market, the experts disagree on the benefits of splits for investors. Following is a point/counterpoint discussion.

Point. Some experts tout the virtues of investing in companies that they think may split their stocks. This brand of "expert" tends to be more short-term oriented and focused on what is working on Wall Street today and not necessarily what works on Wall Street over time.

Counterpoint. During irrational times, any expert can talk about how you can play a stock for its potential of a split, which is just another sign that you might be in irrationally bullish times. At the height on the dot.com bubble, a stock would simply announce a stock split and the next day the stock would rise 30 to 50 percent. And why? Because of nothing more than a split.

My Two Cents. Honestly, there's nothing wrong with companies splitting their stocks. But it's the oldest smoke-and-mirrors trick in the book because it does little more than make a stock look cheaper than it really is. You might not be a great investor if you are impressed with stock splits. Everything else in the company, right down to earnings per share, is adjusted to reflect the split. Nothing—and I mean nothing— changes but the perception of value.

SHORT SELLING

Okay, it must be time to offend the cat lovers. Just as there is more than one way to skin a cat, there is more than one way to make money on a stock. Selling short is one way investors make money on stocks that they believe are going to decline in price in the near future. The important thing to remember: Shorting, while offering a smart way to make bearish bets, carries significant downside risks. Knowing the risks is as important as knowing the rewards. (Sadly, we humans have a tendency to only focus on the upside potential)

To sell a stock short, you borrow the shares from your broker, then sell the shares and hold the money and wait for the stock to fall. If it does, you buy the shares at the lower price and give them back to your broker, who gets a commission and interest for his or her troubles.

For example, assume you borrow 100 shares of XYZ, at $100 a share from your broker, then sell them for $10,000. Let's say the stock drops 20 percent to $80 a share; you buy the shares back for $8,000, then return them to your broker and pocket your $2,000 profit (minus your broker's commission and interest, of course).

Now, let's examine the other side. If you short a stock whose price rises, things can get hairy. (Note: Hairy is never good unless it's the hair on top of your head and you're trying your best to keep it.) You can either wait to see if the stock will decline, which means you rack up hefty interest costs; or, you buy the shares back at a higher price than you sold them, and give them back to your broker (along with the other fees), and take the loss. Covering your short position at a loss can get ugly during a short squeeze. A squeeze occurs when a stock that has been shorted by many investors rises. More and more short-sellers must buy shares to cover their short position, putting greater upward pressure on the stock price.

Professional Opinion on Short Selling

Most individual investors are fascinated with the idea of betting against a company and shorting the stock. Shorting is essentially the mirror image of going long. (Professional investors use the term going long to mean buying with the idea that a stock will go up.)

When you buy, you take it for granted that the stock you buy will be delivered to you. When you sell the stock, you get the difference between the price you paid and the price for which you sold it. Your stock is returned automatically to the buyer.

Short-selling works the same way. You sell the stock. You buy it back, or "cover," and you get the difference. If it went higher, you lose; if it went lower, you made money.

There is one difference however, and it's a doozy. When you buy a stock, you know it is going to be delivered to your account. When you sell it short, you don't own the stock, so there is no surety to the process.

THE HISTORY OF BULL AND BEAR

The symbols don't seem to match—why not just call an up market a hot market and a down market a cold market? Where did the terms bull market and bear market come from? One of the first explanations for the terms that I heard was that they were derived from the way those animals attack a foe. Bears attack by swiping their paws downward while bulls toss their horns upward. Although that is a true description of how they attack, it is not the true origin of the terms.

Another explanation comes from the bear skin jobbers of the old frontier. They were infamous for selling bear skins that they did not own (i.e., the bears had not yet been caught). This term eventually was used in trading to describe short sellers because they did not own the shares they were betting would go lower. Instead, they were hoping to buy them after a price drop and then deliver the shares to the owner. Obviously, these bears were hoping the market would go down.

Because bull and bear baiting were once popular sports, bulls came to be seen as the opposite of bears. Thus, the bulls were those people who bought in the expectation that a stock price would rise, not fall.

Yet another explanation of bulls and bears comes to us from Old England. As far as I can determine, bull and bear were explained for the first time in an English book called *Every Man His*

Own Broker, or, A Guide to Exchange Alley, by Thomas Mortimer, printed in 1785. (London's eighteenth century Wall Street was called Exchange Alley.) Mortimer's book was intended as an inside guide to trading for the common man.

According to Mortimer's definitions, it would appear that bull and bear had much more specific meanings in 1785 than they do today. A bull wasn't just someone who thought—and hoped—that the market would go up. He was the equivalent of a modern day hard-core, chart analyzing, CNBC watching, IBD reading investor who used margin to the hilt. The more margin the better! The bull of 1785 bought stocks with no money at all and hoped to sell them at a profit before payment became due.

In Mortimer's words,

> *. . . a man who in March buys in the Alley 40,000 pounds [of stocks for settlement] in May, and at the same time is not worth ten pounds in the world . . . [he] is a Bull, till such time as he can discharge himself of his heavy burden by selling it to another person, and so adjusting his account, which, if the whole house be Bulls, he will be obliged to do at a considerable loss; and in the interim (while he is betwixt hope and fear, and is watching every opportunity to ease himself of his load on advantageous terms, and when the fatal day is approaching that he must sell, let the price be what it will) he goes lowering up and down the Stock Exchange, and from office to office; and if he is asked a civil question, he answers with a surly look, and by his dejected, gloomy aspect and moroseness, he not badly represents the animal he is named after.*

In Mortimer's day, a bear wasn't just a pessimist; he was a short-seller. A bear was a person who:

> *. . . has agreed to sell any quantity of the public funds more than he is possessed of, and often without being possessed of any at all, which, nevertheless, he is obliged to deliver against a certain time: before this time arrives, he is continually going up and down seeking whom, or. . . whose property he can devour; you will find him in a continual hurry; always with alarm, surprise, and eagerness painted on his countenance; greedily swallowing the least report of bad news; rejoicing in mischief, or any misfortune that may bring about the wished-for change of falling the stocks, that he may buy in low, and so settle his accounts to advantage.*

Mortimer claimed that you could tell bulls and bears apart just by looking at them. He wrote:

> *[The Bear] is easily distinguished from the Bull, who is sulky and heavy, and sits in some corner with a melancholy posture: whereas the Bear, with meager, haggard looks, and a voracious fierceness in his countenance, is continually on the watch, seizes on all who enter the Alley, and by his terrific weapons of groundless fears—and false rumors—frightens all around him out of property he wants to buy; and is as much a monster in nature, as his brother brute in the woods.*

Finally, it was cartoonist Thomas Nast who popularized the modern-day bull and bear as symbols for the stock market's movement. But perhaps it is most appropriate that we end the chapter about stocks and investing with the old but still relevant Wall Street adage: Bulls make money; bears make money; pigs get slaughtered. Don't get greedy!

GETTING STARTED WITH BONDS

THE BACKGROUND ON BONDS

Bonds were very unsexy for most investors in the 1990s. *Business Week* magazine actually went as far as to question whether bonds any longer had a place in the New Economy. However, it was bonds that saved most diversified investors when the stock market tanked in 2000. Do not underestimate the place of bonds or fixed income in your portfolio.

Corporations and governments are just like you and me—every now and then, they need to borrow a little cash. The nice thing about the U.S. government is that we know they are going to spend more money every year than they bring in. They finance their shortfalls by issuing bonds. By buying a bond, you spot the government money. And here's the good part: Unlike when you loan friends money, corporations and governments typically pay you back on time, with interest. Nice deal, right? In fact, the United States government has never missed a payment on a bond.

125

For investors, the big appeal in buying bonds is predictability. They pay interest at a fixed rate for a fixed term. While bonds' performance often lags behind stocks, bonds are considered a safer investment because those fixed payments limit the downside. Bond investing may seem complicated, but the basic idea isn't: You lend your money, you get fixed interest payments over the term of the loan, and then you get your money back at the end. You will learn that predictability and consistency are two important facets of successful long-term wealth building.

There is a wide variety of bonds available today:

- Treasury bonds
- U.S. government debt securities
- Corporate bonds
- Debt securities issued by companies
- Municipal bonds
- Debt securities issued by local and state governments
- Convertible bonds (debt that can be converted later into company stock)
- Junk bonds (debt that offers much higher interest rates because companies have a much higher likelihood of default)
- Mortgage-backed securities (bonds backed by real estate mortgage payments and guaranteed by agencies such as Fannie Mae)

In a nutshell, here's how bonds work:

A company or government issues a bond with a fixed maturity date, which is when the bond comes due and the principal portion of the loan must be paid back in full. The term of the bond can be short term (less than one year), intermediate term (two to ten years), or long term (more than ten years). Typically, the longer the term, the higher the interest rate offered to investors. A bond's interest rate also varies depending on market conditions and the level of risk involved. Bonds are assigned bond ratings by agencies such as Standard & Poor's and Moody's Investors Service according to their risk levels.

A bond's principal amount is its face value—usually $1,000 or some multiple of $1,000. Brand-new bonds are sold at or near par, or 100 cents on the dollar of face value. Bonds pay lenders interest on the principal, usually twice a year; then, at the end of the term, investors get their principal back. The rate of the interest payments on the principal is known as the coupon.

Since bonds make fixed payments, does that mean their value remains constant? No, for this reason: A bond's market value is also shaped by ever-changing economic conditions. A bond's interest rate doesn't change, but the rates being offered on new bonds do. If interest rates move higher as a group then the current bond selection tends to underperform as investors sell what they have in pursuit of something paying a bit higher. So if an existing bond's interest rate is higher than the rates available on new bonds of comparable maturity and credit quality, investors will pay more to buy the bond. In this environment, you could go out and sell a bond you bought at par at a premium, sort of like selling a stock for a gain. When the inverse occurs—a bond's interest rate is lower than the rates on comparable brand-new bonds—if you sell the bond, the buyer will demand a discount. A bond's yield is its rate of return on an annualized basis. The price at which you buy a bond determines the yield you get. The less you pay, the higher the yield. The more you pay, the lower the yield.

WHY BOTHER WITH BONDS?

Would you accept a somewhat lower return if it meant considerably less risk? If so, you're in the market for bonds. Lowering risk is basically what bonds are all about.

But watch out: Bonds aren't foolproof. It's possible to lose money in bonds. In 1994, the worst year for bonds in a generation, lots of investors learned that lesson. Interest rates rose so much and so quickly that the paper price losses on many bonds were greater than the income they generated.

But 1994 was probably close to as bad as it gets. Over the long term, bonds have produced healthy returns—much higher than money market funds, and respectable even compared with equities.

A portfolio of stocks and bonds makes more efficient use of risk than a pure stock portfolio, as history has shown over and over again. The basic principle is this: Adding bonds to a stock portfolio lowers its return—but not as much as it lowers its volatility.

The difference is measured by something called the Sharpe ratio. The Sharpe ratio calculates the difference between the return on an investment and the return on a risk-free investment (Treasury bills, for example), and divides it by the investment's standard deviation, the most common measure of volatility. The ratio tells you how much excess return the investment has delivered per unit of risk.

According to an analysis by Ibbotson Associates, from 1972 to 1997, a portfolio consisting entirely of the S&P 500 returned an average of 13.1 percent a year, while a portfolio consisting of 25 percent intermediate-term government bonds and 75 percent stocks returned an average of 12.2 percent a year. Be careful though; you can not just look at the average rate of return as there is more to the story. More on this in a little bit.

The more diversified portfolio came with less risk. Less risk means you stress less and don't have to deal with fear and greed as often. The stock-bond portfolio generated a Sharpe ratio of 0.44, compared with a lower 0.43 for the all-stock portfolio, indicating that it generated as much return per unit of risk. In fact, it generated a tiny bit more. It's that same return on a smaller amount of risk that prompts Charles Schwab Chief Investment Officer Steve Ward to call diversification "the only free lunch."

There are other reasons besides risk-cushioning for investing in bonds. They are the mainstay investment vehicle for late in life, when you're done accumulating capital and need a steady stream of income. Depending on where interest rates are when you retire, you might go with a more conservative portfolio of bonds or a more aggressive allocation. Bonds are also a strong option for saving. If you know you're going to need a sum of money on a particular date in the future—to pay college tuition bills, for example—you can buy bonds that will come due at those times. In general, bonds serve as protection from the vicissitudes of the stock market.

Now for the bad news: As much as bonds are supposed to be the stable, low-risk portion of your portfolio, the world of bond investing is still rife with pitfalls. Consider the following:

- You can't just buy bonds and assume you have a low-risk investment. Bonds are complicated instruments compared with stocks, involving credit risk (the risk the issuer will default), and interest-rate risk (the risk that interest rates will rise, making bonds issued when rates were lower worth less).
- No bond is immune from interest-rate risk. But in general, bonds with longer maturities carry more of it. So it's possible to take a lot of risk with bonds, not only with low-grade (low quality) corporate and emerging-market issues, which have prices that can drop sharply in economic downturns, but also with issues of the highest quality because of interest-rate risk.

- It's hard to know whether you're getting a good price. If you buy individual bonds as opposed to bond fund shares (which you should do only if you have upward of $25,000 to invest in bonds at the very least, unless you're buying Treasuries), you need to make sure you don't overpay. With stocks, your broker gets a commission. With bonds, instead of a commission, you pay an undisclosed markup on the price of the bond. What's important to you is how the final price you are paying compares with what other investors are paying for the same security. Buying bonds with a high markup makes the investment less attractive.
- Pricing data tends to be catch-as-catch-can, even for institutional investors with lots of money to spend, because virtually all bonds trade over-the-counter rather than on an exchange. And because many bonds are infrequently traded (individual investors typically hold bonds till they mature), prices based on recent transactions often don't even exist. For highly liquid Treasury bonds and notes, prices are widely publicized. But the Treasury market is the exception to the rule.

Two points are worth noting:

- If you buy bond funds, the low returns relative to stock funds means fees and expenses eat up a bigger share. You need to watch fees and expenses as a stock fund investor, but you really need to watch them as a bond fund investor.
- Bond investing has a raft of tax implications. Municipal bonds are federally tax-free and state tax-free if you buy bonds issued in your state. Treasury bond interest is state tax-free, but other U.S. government bond interest isn't. And then there's the alternative minimum tax, which applies to some municipal bonds.

BOND FUNDS

Bond funds offer investors an easy way to tap into the bond market without having to tap too deeply into their savings. Bond funds are a lot like stock funds in that you are hiring professional management to put together a professional portfolio of bonds for you.

We have established bonds are debt that governments and corporations take on. People who buy the bonds are essentially lending money (think professional IOU), which they get back in return plus interest, providing what is generally a fixed-income return. But bonds can be expensive for investors, with the minimum investment often $5,000 or more. The benefit of bond funds is that the minimums for investing are typically lower, and since they invest in a number of offerings, investors get greater diversification.

Bond funds differ from bonds in other ways as well. Unlike individual bonds, bond funds don't have a fixed maturity date, nor do they have a guaranteed interest rate. Also, unlike bonds, bond funds don't guarantee to return your initial investment.

As with stock funds, bond funds come in all shapes, sizes, investment criteria, and risk levels. Some bond funds invest in very safe government bonds that provide steady returns with little risk. On the other side of the spectrum, some bond funds invest in junk, or high-yield, debt from companies. Junk bonds carry a higher risk that the company will default on its loan payments.

Treasury Bonds

Few things in the investing world are considered virtually free of risk, but high on that short list are Treasury bonds.

Treasury bonds are debt issued by the U.S. government. They are issued in $1,000 denominations and mature in anywhere from three months to 30 years. For investors, Treasury bills (which mature in three months to one year), notes (maturing in two to 10 years), and bonds (maturing in 30 years), serve two very important functions. First, as an investment opportunity, they offer fairly low but secure return rates, or yields. Second, Treasuries, especially the benchmark 10-year Treasury note, serve as a primary indicator of interest rates, which are a major influence on the overall economy.

First, let's examine Treasuries as an investment opportunity. Treasury bonds are considered the ultimate in safety; the risk of default is practically nonexistent. During times of uncertainty in the stock market, investors often take money out of stocks and put it into Treasuries, which is often called a flight to quality. In addition to the comfort they provide, Treasuries also outperform other, higher-yielding bonds during times of economic weakness and the interest payouts are exempt from state income taxes. So if you are one who worries a lot or you and your spouse stress about money, maybe Treasuries are a good compromise.

How does one gauge how Treasury bonds are performing? By a Treasury's price and its yield, which move inversely to one another. This is not the easiest concept to visualize but work with it and it will make sense. When they are first offered, Treasury bonds are sold at par, or 100 cents per dollar of face value. But subsequently, they may be bought and sold in the market at prices below or above that level, depending on current interest rates, or yields. The higher the price paid for a Treasury, the lower its yield. The lower the price paid, the higher the yield.

Market watchers also keep a close eye on Treasuries as a proxy for all U.S. interest rates. Treasuries are an important component of a sound investing strategy, whether you buy and sell them or merely monitor their movements as an economic indicator. I am the sort of nerd who tracks a lot of data. The 10-year Treasury is a great indicator to gauge the strength of the U.S. economy. I tend to buy more stocks/fewer bonds when the rate is at 4 percent and fewer stocks/more bonds when the rate is above 5 percent.

Corporate Bonds

Corporate bonds are issued when a company needs to raise money to finance its business operations or, oftentimes, to expand into new directions. In the bond-investing world, they stake out a comfortable middle ground: Their yields, or rates of return, are higher than ultra-safe Treasuries but lower than risky junk bonds.

Corporate bonds have received investment-grade status based on their bond ratings from the major rating agencies, Standard & Poor's and Moody's Investors Services. (Investment-grade status means the corporate bonds received at least a triple-B rating from one or both of the agencies. We'll talk more about bond ratings in the next section.) While not as airtight as Treasuries, which are backed by the government, investment-grade corporate debt is pretty insulated from the risk of default.

These securities, unlike lower-yielding municipal bonds (and Treasuries, which aren't taxed at the state level), are fully taxable.

To buy into a corporate bond offering directly, you have to go through a broker and pay commission fees. But it's very difficult to know whether you're getting a fair price. You also can invest in bond funds that specialize in corporate bond issues.

Even if, as an investor, you choose not to invest in corporate debt, it's an area worth paying attention to. If you are a stock investor, an important facet of a company's financial health is the amount of debt it assumes and its ability to pay it off. To learn about a company's debt you will need to go over the financials. You can find financials inside of the company's annual report (10-k filing), quarterly reports (10-q), or through other sources (like Valueline).

Junk Bonds

When an investment carries a moniker like junk bonds, there's going to be a catch. The name junk does not imply high quality like the word bond does.

Bonds are considered IOUs and junk bonds have some of the highest rates of returns attached to them. The catch in this instance is the risk of default, meaning there's a good chance the companies issuing the junk bonds may fail to make interest payments or repay the loan when it matures. Because of the risks, junk bonds offer higher interest rates to investors, which translate to higher returns, or yields. For that reason, they are also called high-yield bonds in more polite circles.

Who decides if they are junk? The services that offer bond ratings, the big two being Standard & Poor's and Moody's Investors Services. Junk bonds carry ratings below triple-B, or speculative-grade ratings (again, we'll talk more about this in a minute). A company's debt may be considered junk-bond status for a variety of reasons, such as if the firm has weak balance sheets or if it is very small or in a speculative industry.

So, what should you do with all this junk? Many advisors suggest that individual investors should avoid buying directly into junk bonds because of the risk that they will lose big. A safer way to play the junk market is to buy a mutual fund that focuses on junk bonds. Mutual funds offer more diversification and thus can be a safer way of playing into riskier or more volatile investments.

Convertible Bonds

Convertible bonds don't fit neatly into a category. Are they bonds, or are they stocks? Well, the answer is that they can be both. Confused? Don't be.

Convertible bonds are souped-up versions of corporate bonds. Here's how they work: A public company issues the securities, which pay interest at a fixed rate (like a traditional bond), although the rates are generally lower than what standard corporate bonds offer. But when the bonds mature, investors have the choice of either taking the cash or converting the bond into the company's common stock.

Convertible bonds, in effect, offer a safer, alternative way to invest in a company's stock that spares you some volatility. When a stock's price rises, so does the price of the convertible bond. But if the stock price falls, the convertible bond's price drops less than the underlying stock. In a worst-case scenario where a company goes bankrupt, it is the bond holders who get paid before the stockholders do.

Cost considerations, including tax and transaction costs, can eat into the convertible bonds' return. But in a volatile market, investors may decide the extra insurance that convertible bonds provide may be worth the added costs. Investors looking to make a broader bet on convertible bonds may look into bond funds that have a big stake in convertibles.

Municipal Bonds

When it comes to pretax returns, municipal bonds are just about the paltriest investment opportunity out there, getting beaten by Treasuries and corporate bonds. But they have one great feature that keeps many investors coming back for more: The exemption from federal income tax.

Municipal bonds, also known as munis, are debt securities issued by states and local governments looking to raise money to build new roads, schools, or to pay for other initiatives. The interest paid to investors over the course of the municipal bond is tax free at the federal level. And, if the investor resides in the city or state that issued the debt, state and local taxes are normally waived as well. However, if you sell the muni for a profit, the capital gains from the sale are taxable.

Because of their tax-exempt status, munis are a popular investment vehicle for wealthier folks, whose high tax bracket gives them incentive to minimize their tax damage. But for investors in other income brackets, there may be a better solution than munis. These investors may be able to find taxable bonds that offer yields (less taxes) that outdo the yields on a tax-free municipal bond.

Muni bonds, which may have maturity dates more than 50 years away, come in two types. The distinction arises from how the municipality pays the interest on the debt. The first type is called a revenue bond. This brand of muni makes interest payouts from a revenue stream such as highway tolls. General-obligation municipal bonds, like Treasuries, are backed by the ability of the issuer to levy taxes, if necessary, to pay the interest and repay the loan.

The mutual fund industry has been quick to tap the investor interest in modest but tax-exempt returns of municipal bonds. There are many muni bond funds from which to choose, including funds that focus on munis from within a single state. These funds are not only tax free at the federal level, but also at the state and local level for residents. There are now iShares and exchange traded funds that offer investors a chance to tap into a group of municipal bonds without having to do a ton of homework.

What Is an ETF?   An exchange-traded fund (ETF) is a type of investment company whose investment objective is to achieve the same return as a particular market index. An ETF is similar to an index fund in that it will primarily invest in the securities of companies that are included in a selected market index. An ETF will invest in either all of the securities or a representative sample of the securities included in the index. For example, one type of ETF, known as Spiders or SPDRs, invests in all of the stocks contained in the S&P 500 Composite Stock Price Index. But buying an ETF does not mean that you are buying shares of a company; ETFs are shares of a portfolio designed to closely track the performance of any one of an array of market themes and styles of indexes.

An ETF, like any other type of investment company, will have a prospectus. Read the prospectus to learn the goals, risks, and costs associated with that ETF. All investors that purchase shares of an ETF will receive a prospectus unless you have told your broker to not send you anything via the mail.

The Web site of the American Stock Exchange provides more information about different types of ETFs and how they work. You can also find detailed information about ETFs on the Web site of the Nasdaq Stock Market.

What Are iShares? iShares are the world's most extensive family of Exchange Traded Funds (ETFs). iShares combine the advantages of stocks with those of index funds. Like stocks, they are liquid, easy to use, and can be traded in whatever number of shares you wish. Like index funds, they provide diversification, market tracking, and low expenses. In short, iShares are investment tools you can use to get the exposure you need, at the level you want, at the moment you need it.

iShares trade on the American Stock Exchange and the New York Stock Exchange in the same way as shares of a publicly held company. It's easy to buy and sell iShares through any brokerage account. They can be traded anytime during normal trading hours, using all the portfolio management approaches associated with stocks (market orders, limit orders, stop orders, short sales, and margin buying for example). But iShares aren't shares of a company; iShares are shares of a portfolio designed to closely track the performance of any one of an array of market indexes.

iShares are solid, flexible instruments that provide diversification and market tracking performance with low fees and tax efficiency. What's more, with more than a 100 different iShares funds available (stock and bond funds, value and growth, large-cap, and small, domestic and foreign, industry, and sector), they can bring these advantages to every part of a portfolio. Corporations, pension funds, and other large institutions have invested millions of dollars in iShares—and they're available for individual investors too.

MAKING THE GRADE: BOND RATINGS

If you're going to invest in bonds, you have to understand the bond ratings. Before we begin delving into bond ratings, let me make clear that bond ratings do not necessarily reflect the financial health of the company. Oftentimes, the general public finds out about financial weakness of a company long before the credit agencies downgrade the debt.

Since the primary function of bonds as an investment vehicle is to make fixed payments, it's essential that the company or government issuing the debt have the ability to make all payments on time and in full. Bond ratings evaluate the debt issuer to determine the risk of default.

Here's how bond ratings work: The leading rating agencies, Standard & Poor's and Moody's Investors Services, assign ratings when a bond is first issued, and that rating helps determine how high the bond's interest rate will be. If the agencies assign a high rating, that means there's little risk of default, thereby allowing the issuer to obtain a lower interest rate.

The rating agencies assign ratings to all kinds of bonds—debt issued by corporations as well as bonds issued by foreign governments and U.S. municipal bonds issued by states and localities. Even Treasury bonds issued by the U.S. government have ratings, though they're not generally noted since the risk of default is considered negligible.

The agencies review their ratings on a regular basis to determine if the risk of default has changed over time. If they feel that the level of risk has changed, the agencies may downgrade or upgrade a rating. In addition to having an impact on bond prices, corporate bond rating changes can have a big affect on the issuer's stock price. Likewise, an upgrade or downgrade of a developing nation's debt can spur big moves on that country's stock market.

While the rating systems of Moody's and S&P differ somewhat, they're more alike than different. Both agencies have investment-grade ratings, which connote a high level of creditworthiness, and speculative ratings, which mean higher risk levels that merit higher interest rates.

Here are Moody's ratings, from highest to lowest. Investment grade: Aaa, Aa1, Aa2, Aa3, A1, A2, A3, Baa1, Baa2, Baa3. Speculative grade: Ba1, Ba2, Ba3, B1, B2, B3, Caa1, Caa2, Caa3, Ca, C1.

Here are S&P's ratings. Investment grade: AAA, AA+, AA, AA−, A+, A, A−, BBB+, BBB, BBB−. Speculative grade: BB+, BB, BB−, B+, B, B−, CCC+, CCC, CCC−, CC, D.

The Ratings Game

A rating downgrade or upgrade on a company's debt can have a big impact on the company's stock, so it's best to check for the latest moves. Debt allows organizations to do things that they otherwise wouldn't be able or allowed to. Companies use debt in many ways to leverage their business model. If a company has a good credit rating then they get access to cheaper money and with that they can hire more employees, create more research, build more offices, etc. Thus, a company with a good credit rating may find it easier to stay competitive especially if other companies within the sector have poor credit ratings. One of the problems that arises with this type of assumption is that companies with poor credit are worse investments because of the higher cost of money. Sometimes a company will use alternative debt financing or simply sell off assets in order to improve financial strength and creditworthiness.

GETTING STARTED
WITH MUTUAL FUNDS

The three most important tenets of planning an investment portfolio are: diversification, diversification, and diversification. But diversifying when buying stocks isn't cheap, which makes it tough for the individual investor. Often I am asked how much money someone should have before buying individual stocks. My answer is at least $100,000 in liquid assets so that you can get proper diversification. I have learned that most smaller investors want individual stocks, whereas the wealthier a person already is, the more they want to protect their assets through diversification. As with most dilemmas in life, a product has been created to address the problem: the mutual fund.

A mutual fund holds a group of stocks, bonds, or other investment vehicles and is managed by an advising company. In buying a mutual fund, you get to hold a broad range of stocks and/or bonds because your money is thrown into a much larger pot of money from other investors. The upshot: For a modest sum, you get a professionally managed portfolio. Getting a professional to do your homework and buy the stocks seems pretty cool in my mind.

The problem though, is that there is no one fund that fits all sizes so you the individual still have to make decisions. Not all mutual funds are created equal. In fact, some mutual funds with very narrowly focused investment strategies wouldn't meet most people's standards of diversification. So, you, the investor, must understand the many ways in which mutual funds vary in order to best determine which one(s) fits your investment goals.

In the pool of funds there are many different investment objectives, and each carries a different level of risk. In the shallow end of risk, there are mutual funds that invest in currency or government-backed Treasuries that offer unspectacular but steady returns. In the deep end, there are mutual funds that put all their cash into one volatile sector of the market, such as Internet stocks. And in between there are thousands of mutual funds offering various investment objectives, focuses, and risk levels.

Another important matter when considering which mutual fund to buy: How much are you paying the advisor to manage your money? First, there is the question: Does the mutual fund have a load, or sales charge, or is it a no-load offering? Beyond management fees, there may be distribution fees and redemption fees, not to mention expenses associated with stock trades made by the mutual funds. (We will get more into the particulars of each type of fee later in this chapter.) Mutual-fund companies detail their funds' costs in the prospectus, and fees are a major consideration. Don't let fees eat your returns alive.

WHAT'S THE BEST ADVICE ON HOW TO CHOOSE FUNDS?

Whenever I talk to investors, I am continuously pummeled with what I call "The What's?": What's the best stock? What's the best short-term trade? What's the best mutual fund?

The problem is that the question, "What's the best fund?" doesn't have a one-word reply. It can't. Therefore, my usual answer is that I don't know, but I will give you some insight on the funds.

Do Your Homework

Daunting as the list of over 6,000 equity funds may seem, if you're an investor who is willing to spend a little time investigating your investments, you can find the cream of the crop by following a few simple rules. I am only going to concentrate on equity funds, though similar principles apply to the bond portion of your portfolio. Take notes!

Let's start by rephrasing the initial question. More relevant than "What's the best fund?" is, "What are the best funds for me at this time in my life?" And before you answer that, you need a portfolio strategy, or an overall road map.

Map reading is a skill that can drive you crazy. It is really important that you grasp the concept of having a map for your investments so that you know where you are going. Otherwise you might accumulate some assets that work for you short-term but leave you with dramatic underperformance over the long term.

You need to know what purpose each investment vehicle serves in your portfolio. Funds will work hard in different ways and over different territory to achieve your ultimate investing goals. Think of a grid that has style along one axis (value to growth) and size along the other (large- to small-cap). Morningstar divides it into neat boxes and calls it the "style box" and it looks like a tic-tac-toe box.

Where you concentrate most of your money on that graph depends on the basics particular to you—savings goals, time horizon, risk tolerance, view of the future. And don't just check the annualized three-year number. Look at how the fund performed each year and compare it to what happened in the economy, stock market, and other similar funds. You probably don't want a fund that had one rip-roaring year and is now riding on its reputation. Remember that picking the right investment is more about your asset allocation needs than about being right.

Always check, too, that the current manager is responsible for those numbers. If a new guy is on board, you'll want to research his background and also find out why the old manager jumped ship. A fund company offers a short bio on the managers. I would go as far as to Google their names and see if any articles have been written from outside sources that can give you some insight into their thought processes and styles.

When you look at performance numbers, keep them in context. A double-digit return last year might look great until that style of investing hits a cold spell and underperforms right after you buy the fund. For example, a lot of growth fund managers did quite well in the late 1990s as growth investing was a hot style, but when 2000 started most of these fund managers lost significant portions of their previous gains and then some.

I prefer to evaluate performance against peers. How does a fund stack up against those that practice a similar style? Of course, there are drawbacks here, too. If you define peers as funds that have the same investment objective as defined in the prospectus, you won't get very far. These classifications are so broad—capital appreciation, for example—as to be almost meaningless. Morningstar provides a more detailed system and performance numbers can be found from Lipper Analytical Services for a wide variety of time periods.

Consider Costs

I don't blame you for ignoring what your fund costs. No simple sticker serves as price tag, and with a jargon-packed alphabet soup of share classes and load tables, you can go cross-eyed trying to do what any intelligent consumer considers a basic: paying attention to what you're paying.

But costs really are key to future returns. You can't guarantee that your fund will keep racking up the same returns, keep its management, or maintain a set level of volatility. You can, however, know with a reasonable degree of certainty what you will pay.

First, check in your fund's prospectus for the most overt of the charges: A load is essentially a sales commission paid to an investment broker or advisor. As high as 8½ percent, but usually ranging from 2 percent to 5 percent, these fees can take a big bite out of your bottom line. To put this in perspective, a 5 percent load means that for every $100 you invest the fund manager will keep $5. That can really hurt performance over time, especially if you remember that stocks only average 10 percent returns. On the other hand, sometimes a load can be justified via the unique exposure it can get you. For instance, let's say that you really want to own a fund that invests in India or Russia. What do you really know about those countries and investments within those countries? It is likely that if you were ever to go and buy stocks from companies in those countries, you would get charged an arm and a leg and following the data on your investments would be tougher than you would think. Perhaps in a case like that, it makes more sense to pay a higher load than average.

I personally almost never buy a load fund. Some very fine managers work for load funds, and depending on your investment skill and expertise, you may need help choosing funds. Do-it-yourselfers, however, can find plenty of great funds that don't hit you with this granddaddy of mutual fund fees.

The key debate is not load or no-load, but high expenses versus low. A hefty expense ratio can mean a lot more to the long-term investor than an up-front load. So I try to choose funds that have below-average fees. Check out your prospectus to find your fund's expense ratio (the percentage of a fund's assets deducted every fiscal year for operating expenses). Then compare it with the category average. The average expense ratio for equity funds is 1.44 percent, but fees vary dramatically by class.

Remember Risk

There's no shortage of tools—some sophisticated, others rather crude—that the experts use to try to quantify risk: beta, standard deviation, alpha, Sharpe ratio. None of these academic measures is perfect but, depending again on your time horizon and your stomach's ability to take highs and lows, it may be worthwhile to see how a fund stacks up, volatility-wise.

Once you have your charts and graphs in front of you, remind yourself of your bottom line. Remember: The point of investing is not to avoid risk; rather, it's to understand the risk you take.

A Take on Turnover

Turnover simply means buying and selling and thus connotes activity. Activity creates transactions which create costs. Costs take money away from the fund and thus from the investors. Some active managers are more active than others, and you may pay for that. High turnover of holdings means more brokerage commissions. And if capital gains are realized, you will pay taxes on them each year.

So look in a fund's prospectus for portfolio turnover—that is, the annual rate of a fund's buying and selling activity, or how much of a portfolio is turned over or changed. A turnover rate of 100 means the manager changed the entire portfolio (or that 1 percent was traded 100 times, or 25 percent was traded four times, etc.).

Always be careful when interpreting this number. A high number is not necessarily a bad thing. It is simply one statistic and it is out of context. You need to build a case for investment decisions and turnover should be examined but not taken as the only source of data.

Size Matters

How big is your fund? Size can definitely be a drag on performance, so I always want to know how big my fund is and how fast it is growing. This information can be found on the prospectus under the Net Asset line item. This is especially important if you're looking at a small- or mid-cap fund. It just simply is tougher for a bigger fund to be nimble getting into and out of stocks without having an impact on price. Companies are usually classified as either large-cap, medium-cap, small-cap, or micro-cap, depending on their market capitalization, but the dividing lines are somewhat arbitrary.

Small-Cap $250 million to $1 billion capitalization
Mid-Cap $1 billion to $5 billion capitalization
Large-Cap   Over $5 billion capitalization

Is the Manager's Money Where His Mouth Is?

Just as there is strength in numbers, misery loves company as well. You can't just flip open the prospectus and then call the fund's 800 number for your manager's personal details, but this has become a key question for me. Does my manager trade on his own account, or does he have personal money at risk in the fund? I feel much better if I know he will suffer, too, if the fund takes a tumble. And while many managers do trade on their own accounts, I prefer it when all of a manager's market energy is focused solely on my fund.

Recap

So let's recap: After you've screened for all these considerations—performance, cost, risk, turnover, size, a manager's personal accountability—it should be easy to narrow down that overwhelming list of equity funds to a short list of funds that best suit your investment goals.

Different road maps will come up with different funds, obviously—and will dictate different standards for these criteria. For example, say you use an Asset Allocation model that indicates you need an aggressive growth fund to get where you want to go. You should be willing to accept higher risk and perhaps more turnover (in exchange for higher returns) than you would expect from a large-cap value fund. Be prepared for smaller-sized stocks, though, as many aggressive growth funds will focus on small- or micro-cap issues.

How Many Funds Should You Own?

It goes counter to logic but can there really be too much of a good thing? If one is good, two or three must be better, right? Depending on the size of belly or budget, double helpings of Haagen-Dazs shouldn't do too much damage. But many investors share an indulgence that does take a toll on their financial future: owning too many mutual funds.

It happens to the best of us. Your first year on the job, you choose one fund in your 401(k) based on its terrific track record, then the following year when you're ready to stash away more savings, you see that another fund had a hot 12 months, and you add it to the list. Same goes for your IRA. Same goes for your regular account. Wow, you have a lot of different funds all of the sudden.

Then, with the extra nest egg you're keeping for your child's education, you end up following a similar strategy. Rigid models of asset allocation only add to the impulse. We need long-term bonds, short-term bonds, small-cap international, large-cap global, aggressive growth, micro-cap growth, and on and on. Heck, the media even gets you all pumped up about the hot dot.com fund or the "Death of Bonds," so you add or subtract based on the news. Soon you're collecting funds like baseball cards—with the only common theme being the fact that most of them could, at one time, boast a good performance record.

Try to remember the childhood tale of "The Tortoise and the Hare." Everyone knows that the slow and consistent turtle wins the long-term race and yet in the world of investing most investors bet on the rabbit. Don't be that fool who bets your retirement on the rabbit or "hot" tip.

Regular investing in a lot of mutual funds over time may accumulate some wealth. Of course, we may kid ourselves into thinking that we're serving a higher master: diversification. But it simply isn't true that the more funds you own, the more diversified you are. Many funds may be buying similar types of holdings. That's just the opposite of diversification and that means your returns can end up going nowhere.

So the big question, how many is too many?

You'll find answers on both extremes. One financial planner says, if you choose carefully, you're kidding yourself if you think you need more than one fund. On the other hand, I know a very worldly investor who owns more than 100 funds. A solid piece of investment advice rests somewhere in the middle. Depending on your investing knowledge and ability, if you own from six to twelve funds, that should be plenty.

The main reason to hold multiple funds is to manage your portfolio's risk. The idea is that when one type of fund behaves one way to a market move, another will react contrarily. A bond fund may do well in a different environment than a small-cap domestic stock fund, for example.

The key is to make sure each fund has a distinct focus so they don't overlap. How to do this? Don't count on the sweeping investment objectives listed in a fund's prospectus—these are so broad as to be almost meaningless. I prefer the categories offered by Lipper Analytical Services or Morningstar (remember the tic-tac-toe board that classifies style and objective). You can also check the portfolio holdings, but that can be a time-consuming task and not always a dependable one. Often holdings are outdated by time of publication, especially if a manager has a penchant for trading.

A better method is to compare your funds' R-squared ratings (available from Morningstar). This is a little more tricky and takes practice to understand. The R-squared measures a fund's correlation to an index, like the S&P 500, telling you what amount of a fund's return is based on the return of the index. A rating of 100 means the fund basically duplicated the index, while a rating of ten means you can attribute just 10 percent of the return to the index. If you find that many of your funds are highly correlated to the same index, you're not getting the risk-reducing benefits you want from owning a multi-fund portfolio.

So, which six to twelve fund categories do you choose then? That depends on your specific situation. Someone who hates seeing her investment dip into the negative column once in a while because she's saving for a down payment on a house three years from now will have a very different set of categories than a twenty-something willing to ignore all short-term fluctuations in the hope of a hefty return when he's retired.

And the next time you're tempted to indulge in the hottest new fund, stick your money in the ones you've already carefully chosen instead. Unless you are prepared to follow all of them with an extremely watchful eye, you may find this form of collecting a very expensive pastime.

FUND RISK: NOT JUST A NUMBERS GAME

Investing seems like it should be a science. After all there are so many numbers and so much math involved. There is no science in investing. It's an art. Yet all too often, we make the mistake of assuming that, because so much surrounding our mutual fund is numeric, the buy-and-sell decisions are mathematical. Nothing could be further from the truth, especially when considering that one of the most elusive aspects of a mutual fund is its risk.

Talking the Talk: Some Terms

Let's take a quick tour of some of the tools available to assess your mutual fund's risk (or its close cousin, volatility). We'll look at what's the best way to use them to better understand your investments, and perhaps more importantly, why none of these tools alone will give you a truly full picture of your portfolio.

Beta.   Beta compares a mutual fund's volatility with that of a benchmark (usually the S&P 500 index) and is supposed to give some sense of how far you can expect a fund to fall when the market takes a dive, or how high it might climb if the bull is running hard.

A fund with a beta greater than 1 is considered more volatile than the market; less than 1 means less volatile. So say your fund gets a beta of 1.15; that means it has a history of fluctuating 15 percent more than the S&P 500. If the market is up, the fund should outperform by 15 percent. If the market heads lower, the fund should fall by 15 percent or more.

Personally, I would rather get 10 percent returns over time in a portfolio beta of 1 versus 12 percent returns with a beta of 2. Exposing hard earned money to twice as much volatility as the market average can be stressful and can also make individuals more likely to react to fear and greed. Remember that fear and greed should be considered the enemies of good performance.

But beta, though a useful guide, is far from perfect, especially when used as a proxy for risk. The problem here, as with many risk measures, is the benchmark. For funds that don't correlate well with the S&P 500, such as international or precious metal funds, beta just doesn't tell you much.

Alpha.   Alpha was designed to take beta one step further. It looks at the relationship between a fund's historical beta and its current performance, or the difference between the return that beta would lead you to expect and the return a fund actually gets.

An alpha of 0 simply means that the fund did as well as expected, considering the risks it took. So if that fund with the beta of 1.15 beat the market by 15 percent (or underperformed it by 15 percent when the market was down), it would have a 0 alpha. If your fund has a positive alpha, that means it returned more than its beta predicted. A negative alpha means it returned less. Don't read more into it than that.

The trouble with alpha is that it's only as good as its beta. If the benchmark S&P 500 isn't appropriate to a fund in deriving its beta, then alpha, too, will be imprecise.

Standard Deviation.   Unless you are a mathematician it might be tough to imagine a gauge that is more popular than an Alpha or Beta. It is now time to meet the most popular of the risk measures and one with a distinct advantage over beta. While beta compares a fund's returns with a benchmark, standard deviation measures how far a fund's recent numbers stray from its long-term average. For example, if fund X has a 10 percent average rate of return and a standard deviation of 5 percent, most of the time, its return will range from 5 percent to 15 percent. A large standard deviation supposedly shows a more risky fund than a smaller one.

But here, again, what's problematic is your reference point. The number alone doesn't tell you much. You have to compare one standard deviation with the others among a fund's peers.

A more glaring problem is that the standard deviation system rewards consistency above all else. A fund is considered stable based on the uniformity of its own monthly returns. So if it loses money but does so very consistently, it can have a very low standard deviation—down 3 percent each and every month wins a standard deviation of zero. I don't know about you, but that doesn't signal a risk-free investment to me!

And likewise, a fund that gains 10 percent one month and 15 percent the next would be penalized by a high standard deviation— a reminder that volatility, although perhaps a cousin to risk, itself isn't necessarily a bad thing.

Sharpe Ratio. This formula, devised by Nobel Laureate Bill Sharpe, tries to quantify how a fund performs relative to the risk it takes. Take a fund's returns in excess of a guaranteed investment (a 90-day Treasury bill) and divide by the standard deviation of those returns. The bigger the Sharpe ratio, the better a fund performed considering its riskiness.

Here, again, you have the problem of relativity—the ratio itself doesn't tell you anything; you have to compare it with the Sharpe of other funds. But this ratio has an advantage over alpha because it uses standard deviation instead of beta as the volatility variable, and therefore you don't have to worry that a fund doesn't relate well to the chosen index.

Morningstar Risk Ratings

The mutual fund rating company provides, in my opinion, one of the best views of risk. Morningstar says that what we investors really care about is when our funds lose money, not when they're doing better than the benchmark or than their long-term averages. It measures how often and by how much a fund trails the monthly T-bill rate, and then compares that average loss with that for the investment class.

The average for a class is 1.00, so numbers above that mean a fund is riskier than its peers; anything below 1.00 is considered less risky.

Here are a few examples. If a growth mutual fund has a three-year risk rating of 0.94, that means it's viewed by Morningstar as a bit less risky than other domestic equity funds. However, there could be another growth mutual fund that is rated 1.42, or 42 percent more risky than its peers.

As you can see, there's no shortage of tools. But no one number tells with certainty exactly how much risk we take with the funds we buy.

What I suggest is taking a look at these available guides, then also checking out a fund's track record during specific down times. How did it handle the tough times of the fourth quarter of 1998, the 1999 Asian Flu, the market fall of 2000, the terrorist attacks of 2001, and the recession of 2002?

Jack Bogle, senior chairman of Vanguard, told me, "One needs to be conscious of risk, but not push it to the last decimal point. It's about awareness, rather than mathematics."

Indeed.

FUND MANAGERS

A mutual fund will sink or swim based on the fund manager.

A fund manager is the person(s) responsible for the overall strategy and the specific buying and selling decisions for a mutual fund. The fund manager has to draw up the investment game plan and research the securities that meet the fund's goals. The manager is also the point man that makes the moves into and out of stocks.

For investors, a fund manager's long-term performance should be a major factor in deciding which fund to choose. Whatever type of fund you're looking for (value, technology, small-cap fund, etc.), the criteria for choosing a manager doesn't change: The best fund managers are the ones whose funds have consistently outperformed those of their peers over several years. Another key point: If you're choosing a fund with a special focus, say one of the many Medical Devices Funds, it's best to pick a manager who has achieved success within that arena, and not a Johnny-come-lately who was running a value fund six months ago.

To determine a manager's performance, you can't just look at the performance of the fund, because those returns may be the work of a former manager who has recently moved on. Follow the manager's performance from fund to fund. And once you decide to invest in a fund, keep your eye out for any changes at the helm of the ship. If your manager moves on, and the performance wanes after he or she leaves, you may want to look elsewhere as well.

A growing trend within the fund world is having team managers. Firms have several reasons for doing so: It may discourage the star system that can lead to exorbitant salaries for managers, it may protect them from losing clients if one member of the team leaves for another firm, and it may help to have a team with diverse investing backgrounds. But, so far, there isn't any conclusive evidence touting either the more the merrier approach, or the too many chefs spoil the meal angle. So, for investors, the standard rules apply: Check the manager or managers' record before getting in.

Fund Manager's Background

To get the information you need, you're going to have to dig. Frequently, a fund's prospectus won't offer much in the way of background—perhaps it might present the manager's work experience during the last five years and the length of time he or she has been with the fund. The fund's statement of additional information, or SAI, may not contain much more.

You will have a tough time tracing the performance history of any one individual. Unfortunately, you won't find it all just spelled out somewhere. The Securities and Exchange Commission does permit a fund company prospectus to disclose a manager's performance at a previous employer, but you will rarely see this information unless the manager has had some pretty fantastic success.

If a manager has been with one organization for a long time or, better yet, on a single fund, you should be able to piece together the manager's long-term performance record. You will have to find out a manager's dates of service on each fund (via the phone or the Internet) then check out the performance of those funds using a source like Morningstar. But quite often, a manager previously may have been running private portfolios for which there are no public records of performance.

I urge you to use the Internet as much as possible. A simple Google keyword search on a manager's name might turn up very little. But the plethora of online finance publications can help you track down articles that may have been written about that manager. Your public library may also offer free access to one or more publication databases, such as Dow Jones Interactive, that let you search for previously published articles on a manager. If you want to dig that deep, the trip might be worth it.

If you want even more, get your hands on a mutual fund firm's Form ADV. This standard regulatory filing required of all advisers may provide a few details on a fund manager. Off the record, I have never been able to determine exactly what ADV stands for, but I will continue to look for the meaning.

Call your fund company and ask for Parts I and II of this form and make sure you get the schedules that go along with it. Part I will highlight the firm's disciplinary history and any legal or regulatory problems, while the narrative is in the schedules. The information is often printed in such tiny type that it is nearly impossible to decipher. Get a magnifying glass and read this information carefully.

You can also get the Form ADV by calling the SEC's Public Reference Room at 202-942-8090. The SEC will charge you a fee for copying the document, so ask how much it is going to cost.

FUND EXPENSES

Everyone likes to talk about a fund's performance. But one facet of a mutual fund that often gets the short shift but is worthy of equal consideration is its expenses. A fund's expenses, which cover several fees and costs, are a significant determinant in overall performance. Typically, expenses can be as low as a fraction of a percentage point for index funds or exchange-traded funds or as high as 8 percent or 9 percent for funds that carry a sales charge, or load, because they are sold through a broker or financial planner who gets a sales commission. Do more expensive funds deliver better performance? There's no evidence to support that, so investors won't necessarily get burned for bargain hunting (just don't gloss over a fund's performance record and manager).

There are a number of fees and expenses that a fund may offer, and they are always listed in the prospectus, so investors should check them out. Here's a quick list of some of the charges you might find:

- **Management Fees.** This is what you pay for the management to run the fund. Typically, these fees run from a fraction of 1 percent to more than 2 percent.
- **12b-1 Fees.** These fees, also known as *distribution fees,* pay a fund's marketing bills. Not all funds charge them, so this is a spot where investors can cut costs.
- **Redemption Fees.** It often costs funds time, effort, and money when investors buy and sell the offering. To discourage this,

many funds levy redemption fees on investors who sell out of a fund within a certain period.

TURNOVER, LOADS, AND TAXES

There are other cost matters to consider. If a fund has a high rate of turnover, that will typically result in higher costs because there are expenses associated with trading. Also, whether or not a fund carries a load is a big factor in your bottom line.

Loads have virtually nothing to do with performance; they are used as a sales commission. In fact, many funds are offered as load or no-load funds, with very little or no difference between them, apart from the fact that the firms have brokers helping to peddle their wares. So, choosing a no-load fund over a load fund is a pretty easy way for investors to protect their wallets.

Taxes are also an important consideration when buying a fund. Tax-efficient funds implement strategies, such as keeping turnover levels low or shying away from companies that offer taxable dividends, in order to keep tax costs down.

HOW (AND WHETHER) TO READ YOUR MUTUAL FUND PROSPECTUS

I'll let you in on a dirty little secret. There's something that every financial person is supposed to do, but they don't. Everyone should read prospectuses. Few people actually do.

A prospectus is a legal document offering mutual fund shares for sale, required by the Securities Act of 1933. It must explain the offer, including the terms, issuer, objectives (if mutual fund) or planned use of the money (if securities), historical financial statements, and other information that could help an individual decide whether the investment is appropriate for him/her.

These documents are a tough read and are riddled with legalese. I read what I can tolerate, then I file that prospectus away, in my to-do folder. My to-do folder is a ubiquitous black box that contains random parts of my life—cat toys, theater tickets, old manuscripts. The black box is truly a haven of inquiry. Once a prospectus enters the black box, it is never seen again.

In fact, these documents are not intended to educate investors; instead, they're designed to protect the issuers. I think of them not as the ABCs of a mutual fund, but the CYAs. Lawyers throw in every bit of boilerplate imaginable. And that leaves a big job for us: sifting out the real information from the gobbledygook. There actually is very good stuff hidden amongst the herebys and the therewiths, you just have to know where to find it.

Perusing the Prospectus

Here are the highlights, my one-minute guide to your mutual fund prospectus:

Investment Objective.   You want to know your fund's goals and how it will achieve them. Here, you'll find out the basics, but don't expect an in-depth description. Look to see whether a fund can invest in stocks and bonds, or both, and in what combination, or if the manager has an eye on international as well as domestic equities, or large- as opposed to small-cap stocks.

I usually don't depend on this section to tell me much more than that. There can be a huge disconnect between what a fund is allowed to do according to its prospectus and how the manager really invests. Remember: The prospectus is almost always written to give the manager maximum leeway.

The Expense Table.   This is one of the most important parts of the prospectus. It is the fund's price tag, and although it's not as easy to understand as the ones you'll find on your supermarket shelf, the expense table is key investing information. That's because an easy way to boost your returns is by choosing a fund with low expenses.

First, check for any sales commissions (which, as we discussed, are also known as loads). Then size up the expense ratio. That's the percentage of a fund's assets deducted each year for expenses. It includes management fees, which all funds charge to pay for the basics of business, like overhead, manager salaries, and research.

You may also find a 12(b)-1 fee, ranging from 0.25 percent to 1 percent. About half of all funds charge shareholders annually for marketing and distribution. But sales charges and redemption fees, or brokerage fees and other direct trading costs, are not reflected in the ratio.

If you understand dollar amounts better than percentages, you'll find an expense table that shows how fees will affect the value of a $1,000 investment, assuming the fund returns 5 percent a year.

But these numbers won't mean much to you without some context. The average expense ratio for all equity funds is 1.44 percent. You will also want to compare your expense ratio to the average of the fund's peer group.

Financial Highlights.   Here you'll find out how a fund performed for the last few years. But don't stop there! Although returns are what matter most to your bottom line, there are several other important numbers in this section that may have an impact on how your fund will perform in the future.

Because size can be a drag on performance, I like to see how big the fund is and check the Net Asset line to see how quickly it has grown. An example of this is Fidelity's Magellan Fund, which had a stellar track record until the fund became too widely held and thus too big for the management to steer the assets correctly.

I also look at portfolio turnover, that is, the annual rate of a fund's buying and selling activity, how much of the portfolio is turned over or changed. Remember our previous example: A turnover rate of 100 means that the manager turned over, or changed the whole portfolio (or that 1 percent was traded 100 times, or 25 percent was traded four times, or he left half alone and changed the other half every six months).

Higher turnover usually means higher brokerage costs. Also, if the manager makes money on the trades, he is building up realized capital gains, which may mean a higher tax bill at the end of the year for you. But be careful in interpreting turnover. Again, a high number is not necessarily a bad thing. Some managers are great traders and use trading strategies to your advantage. Don't look for a single set of rules to be your guidelines in investing as too many items are simply relative and need comparing.

Take all of these figures into account when reviewing a prospectus. Doing your homework pays off!

READING THE ANNUAL REPORTS: MY TWO CENTS

Annual and semiannual reports may not compete with John Grisham on your summer reading list, but at least they are more interesting and informative than prospectuses. I always look at the Investment Portfolio section to see a list of holdings and sector allocation. But remember that by the time these reports reach you, the inventory may be quite out-of-date for some funds.

I like annual reports mainly because this is the manager's chance to communicate directly with you about what has happened to the fund in the last 12 months. Many managers offer quite candid appraisals of how they're doing.

I want a manager who will tell me he screwed up and why. Is he honest enough to say why he's lagging behind the benchmark? I also like a manager who's on a streak but isn't afraid to warn that those winning ways won't last forever.

Annual reports also offer a window into the investing strategy of Wall Street's smartest minds. I go way out of my way to order over 200 mutual fund annual reports just so I can get my hands on some of the best free investor literature. If I don't know about a sector or a certain part of the world, then I will order a mutual fund's annual reports that currently cover that area. Think of these reports as free educational information.

Having said that, do keep in mind that as entertaining and educational as these reports often are, they do not tell the whole story.

What You Won't Find in Fund Literature

Here are just a few questions you need to consider when buying a fund. Don't expect to find the answers in either your prospectus or annual report:

* How does a fund compare with its peers?
  You likely won't find an answer, unless, of course, a fund is doing better than the average. You're left to check outside sources such as Morningstar and Lipper for those numbers. The SEC toyed with the idea of forcing fund companies to

include some assessment of risk in fund literature, but it soon dropped this tough and controversial issue.

- How did the fund perform in down periods?

  One of the best ways to judge a fund is to isolate its performance in down periods or bear markets. Call a shareholder representative and ask him about the fund's performance for a time period that concerns you, such as the last quarter, for example.

- Who serves on the board of directors?

  You won't find the names of the men and women responsible for overseeing your fund unless you request a Statement of Additional Information. But it's good to know, because in what seems to be an obvious conflict of interest, the board's chairman and directors are sometimes part of management. Not surprising, then, that such items as fee increases or other items on management's agenda often get rubber-stamped.

- Does the manager personally invest in the fund?

  Putting your money where your mouth is means a lot. Ask the shareholder services representative this question, and continue educating yourself on the curveballs that might lie ahead, as investing is an always-changing environment.

OTHER TYPES OF FUNDS

HEDGE FUNDS

Hedge funds are private investment partnerships for institutions and wealthy individual investors that, unlike mutual funds, are largely unregulated by securities industry cops. This doesn't mean they can break the laws, it just means that they can engage in lots of legal but risky investing strategies.

But, before the non-millionaires tune out, take heart and read on: As we'll see, more and more firms are offering funds with hedge-like characteristics for the masses. But a warning for both rich and poor alike: Hedge funds often tread into very risky waters and what can be gained on the upside over time can be taken away on the downside even faster.

What are the characteristics of a hedge fund? These funds aim for outsized, upside returns, often through a number of fairly sophisticated investment strategies such as short selling stocks (an attempt to profit from a stock's decline by selling borrowed stock in the hopes of buying the stock back later at a lowered price), investing in derivatives (hybrid securities, such as crude-oil futures, whose value is pegged to an underlying investment, such as crude-oil prices), and leveraging (investing borrowed money). They get their name from the strategies, such as simultaneous buying and shorting of stocks, they enlist as a hedge against potential market downturns.

Hedge funds have a high entry barrier: The minimum investment is typically in the seven-figure area. Further, because hedge funds are run by money managers who are (in theory) the best in the business, investors pay a pretty penny in annual expenses, often in the double-digit levels compared with low single-digit fees for regular old mutual funds. In fact, most hedge-fund managers are paid based on their performance, typically putting 20 percent of a fund's profits into their pockets. Remember that means they get paid really well when they get you good returns. It is in their best interests to hit a home run as their salary is tied to them outperforming the markets and not from protecting your assets.

Because of the success of hedge funds (or maybe just because people always want what only the rich people have), many firms are rolling out hedge-like funds that use the same investing strategies. Of course, these funds face greater regulation and disclosure rules than hedge funds, which enjoy the luxury of keeping their investment strategies close to their vest.

For investors dipping into the hedge fund or hedge-like fund waters, it is critically important to know the reputation, investing style, and performance record of your manager. Since this is a game for high rollers, you don't want a greenhorn handling your green.

INDEX FUNDS

Over the long haul, it's pretty tough to beat the market, which historically has churned out average annual returns of about 10 percent. It is from the "If you can't beat 'em, join 'em" spirit, that index funds were created.

Index mutual funds aim to match the performance of a securities index by purchasing shares of all or nearly all of the stocks in that particular index. The granddaddy of all index funds (and still the biggest index fund), the Vanguard 500 Index, was created in

1976 for investors to track the performance of the S&P 500, a broad index that lists 500 large companies from a cross-section of sectors. Since then, index funds have cropped up that mirror just about every index out there: small-cap indices, sector indices, you name it. Indeed, there are even enhanced index funds that try to slightly exceed the performance of a given benchmark, but that isn't always easy to do. (Another growing segment of index funds are exchange-traded funds. More on those later.)

Because the aim of most index funds is merely to mirror an index's performance, the funds aren't actively managed. This means the management fees are typically far less expensive than most mutual funds. Their relatively low cost is a key factor in their popularity.

Keep in mind that index funds don't try to set the world on fire, they only want to match an index. If the benchmark index goes up about 10 percent for the year, so does the index fund. If the benchmark declines 10 percent for the year, guess what the index fund does?

The whole point behind buying an index fund is to own a large piece of the market and—for better or worse—ride it over a long period of time, at least ten years. You don't know which stocks will outperform at any given time, so you're buying the entire market. Vanguard's indexing guru Gus Sauter likes to say, "Investing is a marathon, not a sprint." If you want to take a huge bet on a particular sector, you probably don't want an index fund. If you think there's a possibility you may be wrong, you want diversification.

People shouldn't commit 100 percent of their assets to any one single index. You should look for diversification among the indices. It can't be large-cap growth forever, and it can't be tech forever either. Large-cap growth investing worked really well in the last five years of the 1990s but then it was value funds that did well from 2000 through 2005. No one could have predicted that the ten-year period would have been split down the middle like that.

Like all investment vehicles, indexing has its proponents and its detractors. Whether it works for you depends on what you want out of your portfolio. Want to swing for the fences and take on some risk in a bid to beat the pack? Try an actively managed fund. Want to "join 'em," and be content with matching the index of your choice? Look no further.

INTERNATIONAL FUNDS

International funds—funds that focus their investments on overseas markets—are a great way for investors to tap into global economic growth as well as diversify their holdings beyond just homegrown U.S. stocks.

Within the large umbrella of international mutual funds there exists just about every type of mutual fund offered: bond funds, index funds, sector funds, small-cap funds, and so on. Also, investors can choose an international fund that focuses on a single country, a region, or one that includes every foreign country under the sun. (That last category raises a distinction to keep in mind: Offerings known as global funds or worldwide funds typically include U.S. stocks or bonds in their portfolio.)

One of the great things about international funds is that they give small investors access to regional stocks that would be difficult or at least very expensive to buy on their own. Another sound reason to invest in international funds is diversification.

However, plunking down some money for an overseas fund doesn't ensure diversity. Investors need to examine what kind of investment aims a fund has: Does it favor high-octane, high-risk technology stocks? Is it focused on small-cap stocks, or familiar blue-chip multinational stocks? To illustrate the point, the spring 2000 swoon in technology stocks hammered U.S. shares, but it also reverberated among tech stocks around the globe. Having a U.S. fund that invested heavily in tech stocks and an international fund that had a similar sector weighting wouldn't have given an investor a diversified portfolio.

Thanks to international funds, the world can be your oyster, but if you're not careful you can get shucked. It's best to keep yourself abreast of the world of international funds.

International Fund Investors
Seek Long-Term Gains

As the domestic investing scene started to stagnate in the early 2000s, Americans were venturing outside U.S. borders and discovered that international opportunities offered significant returns, particularly over the long haul. The amount of new money flowing into international and global mutual funds has risen at a double digit pace for the past five years.

The money going to international funds still pales in comparison to that going into domestic funds. Nevertheless, the numbers do indicate that investors, including retail investors, are looking outside the U.S. for investment opportunities. The global economic situation has stabilized. The economies of most countries with markets attractive to investors are now posting positive growth.

For the investor looking for the quickie, short-term gain, international funds are not the place to be. However, over the long term, the rest of the world (or at least a lot of it) looks promising.

Benjamin Tobias, president of Tobias Financial Advisors, says "overseas has a lot more upside, a lot more potential" than the United States. He urges investors to look abroad for the long term, at least five years. Investment advisors usually recommend 15 percent to 25 percent of international exposure in their portfolio.

Think about it. Theoretically speaking, the rest of the world is where the United States was, say ten or twenty years ago in both economy and standards of living. There is a lot of international growth coming down the road. You might want to look back at historical returns just to see the future of overseas investing.

EXCHANGE-TRADED FUNDS

Exchange-traded funds, one of the hottest investment trends, are essentially mutual funds that trade like stocks.

As with a typical mutual fund, investors can purchase ETFs and get the equivalent of a portfolio of stocks through a single investment. Also, like typical mutual funds, there aren't a fixed number of ETF shares to be purchased.

However, investors can buy and sell shares of exchange-traded securities throughout each trading day—just like stocks—paying typical brokerage commissions.

Because ETFs track indices, these securities are cheaper than actively managed stock funds. Proponents of these products also praise their tax efficiency, as they tend not to make taxable distributions to shareholders. Since ETFs are cheaper and more convenient than traditional mutual funds, many believe they could start to replace mutual funds as the core holdings in many investors' portfolios.

"They're a brilliant idea, with low costs and potentially a lot of tax efficiency," says Jack Bogle, the former chairman and perennial conscience of index-titan Vanguard. The firm recently filed paperwork with regulators for its own line of index-tracking ETFs, called VIPERs. More information on ETFs can be found at etfconnect.com.

VA VA VOOM: MONEY MARKET FUNDS

Some things will never be considered sexy: Neck braces, car batteries, C-Span, financial books. You can add money market funds to that list.

Money market funds are a variation on a savings account. The good news is that these funds are virtually risk-free—you'll only gain low to mid-single-digit returns, but you won't lose money. Plus, they typically allow you to write checks drawing from the money in your account for no charge. The bad news is you don't get to brag about your money market fund's returns to your friends.

Money market funds invest your money in secure, short-term corporate and government debt such as 13-week Treasury bills and certificates of deposit, or CDs. What do you get in returns? Well, you get your money back for starters, plus whatever interest is earned from the fund's relatively short-term investments.

These funds are a natural fit for older investors who just want to make sure they can preserve their nest egg, while returning modest gains. They also are a safe place to sock away some cash that you plan on using in a few months, say, for a mortgage. Further, some financial advisors suggest keeping a small portion of their holdings—say, less than 15 percent—in a money market fund.

Investors can opt for either a tax-free or taxable money market fund. It sounds like a no-brainer, but there are other differences to consider. Taxable funds typically invest in debt offerings that provide a better rate of return, or yield, than tax-free funds. But, you have to pay taxes on any earnings you make on the investments. Tax-free funds, meanwhile, invest in short-term municipal bonds and other debt offerings that are typically exempt from federal and sometimes state taxes.

Some (Not All) Financial Strategies
for Mutual Funds

1. Have a Roadmap. Choose mutual funds based on financial goals and the expected time frame needed to achieve them.
2. Look for Long-term Performance. Check 3-year and 5-year

returns on funds, not just the last quarter. Compare mutual funds to their peers as well as to a relevant market index.

3. Consider Costs. They are the key to future investment returns. Look at the total expense ratio, not just front-end loads, for a true picture of fees charged to investors.

4. Remember Risk, But Don't Overemphasize It. Compare evaluating a fund's risk level to looking under the hood of a car. Check a fund's record during down markets and note that successful investors don't avoid risks, they understand and manage them.

5. Get a Take on Turnover. This is the annual rate of a fund's buying and selling activity (e.g., 100 percent means the entire portfolio changes during a year). High turnover generally translates into higher taxes as a fund's capital gains are passed on to investors.

6. Size Always Matters. The size of a fund can be a drag on performance. Big mutual funds are like battleships sailing on a small lake. It is difficult for them to maneuver in and out of stocks without having an impact on their price.

7. Check if the Fund Manager Owns Shares. This information is not in a prospectus so you'll have to call the fund itself for details. There may be a measure of security in knowing that the manager's money, as well as your own, is at risk in a fund.

8. Know When to Say When. Some people collect funds like baseball cards, adding today's hot performers to those that were hot previously. Six to twelve funds is enough for most people. Look for listings of funds' top holdings and their R2 (this tells how close a fund tracks a market index) to avoid duplication.

9. Know When to Sell. Times when a sale is in order include: when financial goals change and when you're losing sleep over investment losses. Don't automatically dump a fund when its manager changes but watch resulting performance figures carefully.

10. Relax! Focus on your goals and remember that having any amount of money in investments is better than none even if someone tells you that it is not enough. Will you make mistakes? Of course. Learn from them and move on.

Also, purchase an international fund for diversification and place high-turnover funds in tax-deferred accounts and index funds in taxable accounts.

STRATEGIES, TIPS, HINTS, AND MORE

GET YOUR MONEY WORKING FOR YOU VIA COMPOUND INTEREST

Compound Interest has been called the eighth wonder of the world, the world's most powerful force, and the greatest discovery of all time. Compounding means that interest is paid on interest in addition to the principal. Albert Einstein, well known for being smarter than average, once called compound interest "the greatest mathematical discovery of all time."

The concept is this. When you invest money you earn interest on your capital. The next year you earn interest on both your original capital and the interest from the first year. In the third year you earn interest on your capital and the first two years' interest. The concept of earning interest on your interest is the miracle of compounding.

The difference from simple interest is that the principal balance grows by the amount of interest earned in past periods depending on the stated compounding period; annually, quarterly, monthly, and daily are the most common. The shorter the compounding period, the faster your money will grow.

Annual Compounding

With a method of annual compounding, the amount of interest earned in the first year is added to the principal at the end of the year. During year two, interest will be earned on the total and that will be added to the principal at the end of year two, and so on for the ten years (see Table 13.1):

Table 13.1 The Miracle of Compounding

Time Period	Beginning Balance	Interest Earned	Ending Balance
Year 1	10,000.00	500.00	10,500.00
Year 2	10,500.00	520.50	11,020.50
Year 3	11,020.50	550.13	11,570.63
Year 4	11,570.63	570.88	12,150.51
Year 5	12,150.51	600.78	12,760.28
Year 6	12,760.28	630.81	13,400.10
Year 7	13,400.10	670.00	14,070.10
Year 8	14,070.10	700.36	14,770.46
Year 9	14,770.46	730.87	15,510.33
Year 10	15,510.33	770.57	16,280.89

If you were to let that $10,000 run for 20 years, your profit from the investment would be $16,533 (ignoring taxes). But if you doubled the rate of interest to 10 percent, how much money would you earn?

Although it would seem that doubling the rate would double the return, this is not the case: Increasing the rate by 100 percent increases the return by nearly 350 percent. In other words, instead of earning $16,533 in interest, you would earn $57,275.

That's the power of compound interest: Money doesn't grow linearly—it grows exponentially!

Compounding Works Miracles

As shown in Table 13.2, long-term compounding really is miraculous.

Table 13.2 Growth of $1,000 in Annual Investments

	Annual Growth Rate	
Years	5%	9%
1	$ 1,050	$ 1,090
10	$13,207	$16,560
20	$34,719	$55,765
25	$50,113	$92,324

The Rule of 72

Although you should be pretty comfortable with the effects of compound interest there is also a handy shortcut known as the Rule of 72. It states that you can find out how many years it will take for your investment to double by dividing 72 by the percentage rate of growth. So it will take nine years for your investments to double if they grow at 8 percent per year (72 ÷ 8 = 9). But it will only take six years if your investments grow at 12 percent per year, and so on. The Rule of 72 only provides an approximation, but it is sufficiently accurate for many calculations.

CHECKLIST FOR INTERVIEWING A FINANCIAL PROFESSIONAL

Print this checklist and use it when you are interviewing a financial planner.

Planner's Name:
Company:
Address:
Phone:
Date:

1. Do you have experience in providing advice on the topics below? If yes, indicate the number of years.

Retirement planning

Investment planning

Tax planning

Estate planning

Insurance planning

Integrated planning

Other

2. What are your areas of specialization?

What qualifies you in this field?

3a. How long have you been offering financial planning advice to clients?

❏ Less than one year   ❏ Five to 10 years

❏ One to four years   ❏ More than 10 years

3b. How many clients do you currently have?

❏ Less than 10 clients   ❏ 40 to 79

❏ 10 to 39   ❏ 80 +

4. Briefly describe your work history.

5. What are your educational qualifications?

Give area of study

Certificate

Undergraduate degree

Advanced degree

Other

6. What financial planning designation(s) or certification(s) do you hold?

❒ CERTIFIED FINANCIAL PLANNER™ or CFP®

❒ Certified Public Accountant-Personal Financial Specialist (CPA-PFS)

❒ Chartered Financial Consultant (ChFC)

❒ Other

7. What financial planning continuing education requirements do you fulfill?

8. What licenses do you hold?

❒ Insurance   ❒ Securities   ❒ CPA

❒ J.D.   ❒ Other

9a. Are you personally licensed or registered as an investment adviser representative with a state(s)?:

❒ Yes   ❒ No

If no, why not:

9b. Are you or your firm licensed or registered as an investment adviser with the:

❐ State(s)?   ❐ Federal Government?

If no, why not:

9c. Will you provide me with your disclosure document Form ADV Part II or its state equivalent?

❐ Yes   ❐ No

If no, why not:

---

10. What services do you offer?

---

11. Describe your approach to financial planning.

12a. Who will work with me?

❐ Planner
❐ Associate(s)

12b. Will the same individual(s) review my financial situation?

❐ Yes   ❐ No

If no, who will?

13. How are you paid for your services?

☐ Fee   ☐ Commission   ☐ Fee and commission

☐ Salary   ☐ Other

14. What do you typically charge?

Fee:

Hourly rate $ _____

Flat fee (range) $ _____ to $ _____

Percentage of assets under management _____ percent

Commission:

What is the approximate percentage of the investment or premium you receive on:

stocks and bonds _____

mutual funds _____

annuities _____

insurance products _____

other _____

15a. Do you have a business affiliation with any company whose products or services you are recommending?

☐ Yes   ☐ No

Explain:

15b. Is any of your compensation based on selling products?

☐ Yes   ☐ No

Explain:

15c. Do professionals and sales agents to whom you may refer me send business, fees, or any other benefits to you?

❒ Yes   ❒ No

Explain:

15d. Do you have an affiliation with a broker/dealer?

❒ Yes   ❒ No

15e. Are you an owner of, or connected with, any other company whose services or products I will use?

❒ Yes   ❒ No

Explain:

---

16. Do you provide a written client engagement agreement?

❒ Yes   ❒ No

If no, why not:

FIVE FINANCIAL STRATEGIES FOR YOUR FUTURE

1. Save and Invest Painlessly. Savings and investments should be automated to the extent possible so that you don't need to remember where and when to make deposits. Arrange to have money deducted from your paycheck or bank account. Examples include 401(k), 403(b), or Section 457 employer retirement savings plans. Also think about preauthorized mutual fund deposits that transfer funds from a bank account, and the purchase of U.S. Savings bonds by payroll deduction.

2. Cut Your Debt and Spending. Many Americans have bad spending habits. Good strategies include: Switching to a credit card

with a lower interest rate, avoiding the use of high-interest department store cards, seeking low-rate car loans, and refinancing your mortgage.

3. Cut Your Taxes. Recent tax law changes provide increased incentives to save and opportunities to reduce federal income taxes. Max out your 401(k) to lower your taxable income. Then consider opening a 529 plan for your children's college or Roth IRA so your money will grow tax free.

4. Be a Stock Market Investor. Most mutual funds don't beat market averages and so I recommend putting some money in an index fund that mirrors a market index (e.g., S&P 500, Vanguard Total Stock Market). Two other advantages of index funds: Low expenses and relatively low turnover, which can mean lower taxes.

5. Use Your Computer to Help Manage Your Finances. Popular software programs such as Quicken and Microsoft Money can simplify financial recordkeeping. Online brokerages are another popular trend for consumers who just need to have trades executed and don't require research or advice.

INVESTING MISTAKES: BEHAVIORAL FINANCE

Stop making mistakes and you will automatically play the game better. Play the game better and the investments will take care of you better. Recognize that if your emotions are causing you to act, you are making the wrong decision at the wrong time.

Five Emotions that Hurt Your Financial Goals

The following are five emotions that can knock you off your game. Conquer them.

Fear. A little fear is normal. Fearful investing will cause knee-jerk decisions.

Greed. Had some good returns? Don't get too trigger-happy or you could lose the farm.

Optimism. The sun will come out tomorrow, but the Dow might not.

Pessimism. Balance is good—being a grumpy old miser isn't.

Regret. So you screwed up. Get over it!

If your spouse sees you in any of these roles then you are in trouble.

Let's look a little deeper, shall we? Tell me about your mother…

Fear. Fear is defined as a lack of confidence. Look at history. Since 1940 stocks have risen 77 percent of the time. Yet during that time period presidents have died in office, tensions with Russia led to fears about nuclear war, atomic bombs exploded in Hiroshima and Nagasaki, McCarthy held hearings against purported Communists, and we engaged in a cold war.

Today we have Osama Bin Laden, high oil prices, inflation fears, and terrorism—the list goes on. Yet the band plays on and market has gone up seven out of ten years. The best odds on the planet might be in the market. Spend your energy on your intellect and don't let fear play you.

Greed. Greed is almost as strong as fear.

The market has averaged 12 percent returns for the past 75 years. During the 1980s the markets averaged 15 percent returns and then in the 1990s investors got 25 percent returns.

What will the average be in the next 10, 20 years? 5 percent? 10 percent? 20 percent? If the Dow grows at 7 percent over the next 20 years the Dow will be at 40,000. If it gets 10 percent it will be at 80,000. Both of those numbers are well below what the market did in the 1990s, 1980s, and in the past 75 years. Recognize that small rates of return over time produce dramatically high wealth numbers. Bide your time. Don't get caught up in the media frenzy and don't do something dumb like sell your house or other assets just to get into the market.

The bank gives you 2 percent on your cash. Look at the math when you play with investments. When do most people want to sell a $10 stock? At $20. That is a 100 percent return—it is also greedy. You could only get 2 percent at the bank! Lower your expectations to $12, which is a 20 percent return and a much more realistic expectation.

Eighty-five percent of investors in the most successful mutual fund of all time have lost money. Peter Lynch ran the Fidelity Magellan and 85 percent of the participants lost money as they bought high on greed and sold low on fear.

Optimism. If greed is overconfidence in the market, then optimism is overconfidence in yourself. Here's a test. Ask yourself: Are you funnier than others? Smarter? Do you expect to win all competitions? If you answered yes to any of these then you might be overconfident.

Optimists exaggerate their talents; this can create problems. Too many people think they are better at investing and stock picking. They overestimate their knowledge and make the assumption that they can control events. This type of thinking is very dangerous and all too common. Investing all your money in the company you work for is also very dangerous. Look at the thousands and thousands of people who worked at Enron and Worldcom and had their whole 401(k) in the company's stock. Were they all stupid? Of course not. But they certainly were overly optimistic.

Pessimism. Pessimism is a lack of confidence. Is that you? Can you pick the best stock or best mutual fund? You may think you can't do it and the financial media is right there to reinforce that idea. Don't let pessimism stop you from investing. The worst mutual fund from 1989 to 1999 made more money than the average CD rate during that 10-year period. Creating wealth is about betting on all the horses and funding them appropriately, as the winners will more than compensate for the losers. Stocks, bonds, and mutual funds work over time. Warren Buffet once said that it is better to be approximately right than precisely wrong. Pessimists are pessimists because they fear regret.

Regret. Regret means you wish you had not done something that you have already done and it is an awful feeling. Most people will do anything to avoid regret or making the wrong decision. When it comes to investing, avoiding regret is simple: Do your homework and make the best decision that you can and then never look back on it. Regret is based on looking backward, so don't do it. Check a box and move on.

More Emotions that Can Skew Your Financial Success

Hindsight. Hindsight is the tendency to overemphasize the past—to take what you know now and apply it to how you acted back then. The ability to go backward with hindsight is a very risky proposition.

After an investment performs poorly, we say dumb things like, "I should have seen the Nasdaq collapse coming." I have never met an investor who had psychic powers, but I've met many who think they do. This plays back into optimism and overconfidence. If you think you will do better at investing in the future due to your newfound hindsight, you are merely setting yourself up for more economic disaster.

Quilting. People tend to perceive trends where none exist. For instance, let's say we get eight money managers in a room and in one year, four will beat the other four, right? In year two, two managers will beat the other two. In year three, one manager will beat the last. He can claim he is the best. Investors will see that he had three great years in a row. He must be the All Knowing King of Investing right? Wrong! Is he a genius because he had great returns for three years in a row? Nope. He was merely the benefactor of chance.

We look at Morningstar and Lipper and see there is no correlation between past performance and future results. None. Zippo. Yet we seem to believe that there is—we want to believe there is. Remember the old Psychology 101 maxim: Correlation does not equal causation. Stop seeing what is not there.

Loss Aversion. Loss aversion. What does that mean? Well it simply means that most people dislike losses more than they like gains. Does that describe you? It does me. I'd rather avoid a loss than get a gain. But if you're so afraid to lose money that you don't give yourself the opportunity to make money then, as a result, you will stay poor. Don't fall into this trap. Recognize that if you're going to attempt to achieve wealth, you must take some risk. If you are not willing to take risk, you have no hope of accumulating wealth. *There are no low risk and high return investments.* Recognize that; own it; then move on and find the risk level that works for you.

Accidental Anchoring. Irrelevant numbers mean nothing yet many investors make the mistake of assigning importance to random points. How many different investment choices are there in your 401(k) plan? In most people's company retirement plans, they have five or six choices. When people have five choices, they tend to invest in five different things. When they have ten choices, they tend to invest in ten different things. In other words, people make their investment decisions based on the opportunities in front of them. What you should be doing is deciding how you want your money invested, then manipulating the available choices to meet that goal. Stock prices, PE ratios, car prices, and movie ticket prices are pointless pieces of data toward that end. Stay focused on what counts.

FARMERS VERSUS FOREST RANGERS

Do you know the difference between farmers and forest rangers? A farmer is a person who takes a seed and plants it in the ground, takes a step, plants another seed, takes another step, and plants another seed. Farmers deal with individual trees, focusing on them one at a time. Forest rangers go to the top of the tower and look out over all the trees at the same time—they scan the entire landscape of the forest. In the world of investments, you need to be a forest ranger.

Investment farmers make a lot of bad decisions. This is the problem of the entire personal financial press. Think about it. Every issue of every magazine, every broadcast of every radio and TV show is always focused on the very same thing. They are telling you which hot stock to buy now. They are talking about individual stocks. Do you know what they never do in any of those publications or on any of those broadcasts? They never tell you how much of your money to place into any one of those stocks at any one moment. They are never giving you the whole forest, and that is the key. It's not a question of which particular stock you buy. The question is how much of your money you put into it, versus all the other stocks out there.

Investing has to work in asset allocation, but the financial press doesn't entirely advocate that. The press tells you that you can own this and not that, which sounds like sage advice except it's wildly out of context. Financial decisions need to be made in context of everything else you have like credit card debt, 401(k) savings, college savings, and retirement. Sexy stock tips are shots in the dark that mess up an investor's long-term plan. Lack of awareness, of how one thing affects another, is what leads to financial losses.

So what happens when investors act out of greed or fear? When they display optimism or pessimism, when they see patterns that don't exist, when they tie themselves to anchors, when they fall victim to hindsight and regret, or when they farm instead of invest? Investors who are prone to those emotions and biases will take risks they do not acknowledge, experience outcomes they did not anticipate, will be prone to unjustified trading, and will usually blame others when the outcomes are bad. Do yourself a favor and guard against these mental mistakes.

LOOKING FOR GREAT INVESTMENTS?

The average investor pays a lot of attention to *Forbes, Fortune, WSJ, IBD,* the *New York Times, CNBC, CNN,* Bloomberg, "PBS Nightly Business Report," *Barron's, Business Week,* and *Kiplinger's,* but smart money people don't do any of that. Who wants to read and hear all that boring information anyway? Financial media is as dull as it is misleading. People think they won't make money if they don't listen to the financial media. Nonsense.

Creating wealth is all about having the right mentality. Who will end up with more money—the man who is a great stock picker and an average saver or the average investor who is a great saver? The great saver, of course. Because at the end of the day, it's not what you have made, it's what you have managed not to spend.

The person who diverts the most money into investments is better off than a great stock picker. It doesn't matter if you pick the right investment. It matters how much you have invested. So instead of looking for the hot tips, market manipulations, research, and the like, simply focus on your saving habits.

Warren Buffet, considered the best investor of all time, has said that even the best investors might find only 20 really great investments in their whole life. Yet, all the financial media does is show you hundreds of hot tips per week. Ignore the hot tips. Add money to the accounts you already have. Do this and you will accumulate wealth.

Personal finance is more of a chore than a hobby. Don't buy on tips but do seek good advice on where to put your money. Talk to your parents or wealthy people to get ideas. Although you don't need to disregard the media completely, keep in mind that they give both good and bad advice. Remember, the media's primary job is to sell advertising, not to be your personal investment advisor.

Wealthy People Make a Little Money
Grow into a Lot of Money

If you are poor and you want to be rich, you've got to start doing what rich people do. Wealthy people do not get rich by investing large amounts of money. Rich people get rich by investing small amounts of money.

So, where do they get it? Most wealthy people get wealthy through their own efforts. They work hard. They get an education and a good job. They have kids and work even harder and, through it all, they still manage to save money. They don't start with $100,000. They save regularly through their lives. They add to their savings whenever possible. No matter how much they have, even if it is less than $100, they save some of it. They set money aside in a special account earmarked for savings. They accumulate money and then invest it.

There is no shortcut. Don't let anything stop you from saving.

Wealthy People Rarely Juggle Investments

Quit changing plans. Stay focused. Buy investments and leave them alone. Quit trying to time the market. Forget buy low and sell high. If anyone could do that on a regular basis they would be bazillionaires.

If your investments are all one year old or younger then you are not an investor. You are a trader. How many traders do you know that are millionaires? Personally, I don't know any.

And Now, a Scene from Investor's Theater

Date: 1927

Cast: Two American Investors, named A and B

Storyline: Each Investor has just received $10,000 from the Magic Genie.

Investor A buys stocks in 1927 and holds them for 71 years and gets the average return of the S&P 500.

Investor B sells and moves money around. In and out, in and out. Dumb right?

But here's the catch: The Magic Genie has bestowed Investor B with Perfect Investor Syndrome. Over the years, Investor B has manipulated his money 100 percent perfectly and has cashed in on all the ups and avoided all the downs. Guess what he is worth? $54 trillion dollars. Anyone know any trillionaires?

The Magic Genie was just kidding with Investor B, telling him Perfect Investor Syndrome doesn't exist. Investor B loses the farm.

Investor A, on the other hand, is alive and well. His strategy has earned him an honest $21 million dollars. He's over 100 years old, but with that kind of money, he paid the genie for eternal life.

The moral of this story is that there are no software packages or newsletters that can get you in and out on a regular basis.

For the five years ending December 31, 1997 the market's average returns were 25 percent per year. WOW!!! That was the best five years ever recorded. The entire profit for that five-year period occurred in just 40 days. You think you can tell me which 40 days? Do you think you could have predicted those particular 40 days in advance? If so, you must be Karnack the Magician. You get the point: Stay invested.

401(K) PROBLEMS

Let's recap just a few of the observations made earlier:

- Americans don't save enough for retirement.
- Baby boomers and generation X-ers are not going to be ready for retirement.
- 401(k)s were designed to be *supplemental* retirement plans.

Now, what can you do (and *not* do) to fix this?

Do and Don'ts

- Do save 15 percent of your salary.
- Don't cash out on your retirement plan when switching jobs.
- Do roll plans over so as not to lose your most vital advantage—time.
- Don't take loans against the 401(k) plan. Borrowing from the plan chips away at future retirement wealth.
- Don't make lousy investment decisions, including putting too much money in your company's stock.

25 Basic Principles of Investment

1. Time and a healthy savings rate will solve most investment woes.
2. Your top two financial priorities should be 1.) maxing out your 401(k) plan every year and 2.) paying off your credit-card balance each month.
3. Your employer's stock is the riskiest stock you can own. You already rely on your employer for a paycheck and benefits. Why compound the risk by betting your portfolio's future on the same company?

4. If you invest in just a couple of stocks, the odds suggest you will lag behind the market average. In any year, the market's return is driven by a minority of stocks that post blowout gains. Unless you diversify broadly, you probably won't own any of the big winners.

5. If you will need your money back within a few months, it is foolish to own stocks. But if you won't need your cash for another 10 or 20 years, it's foolish not to own stocks.

6. Investors collectively cannot beat the stock market, because collectively they are the market. In fact, after investment costs, investors—as a group—are destined to lag behind the market.

7. If asked for a market forecast, your best bet is to express cautious optimism, because stock prices rise over time.

8. If you hear a stock touted on television or read about its healthy earnings in the newspaper, the news is probably already reflected in the stock's price.

9. A tumbling stock market may be upsetting. But it doesn't have any financial impact, unless you have to sell. And if you have the money to buy, the sell-off becomes an opportunity.

10. Long-term inflation is a far greater threat than short-term market gyrations.

11. If you don't fully understand an investment, don't buy it.

12. Focus on how much your portfolio makes each year, after making allowances for investment costs, inflation, and taxes. If you are not ahead after taking those three factors into account, you're not making money.

13. At the shopping mall, price may bear some relationship to quality. But on Wall Street, paying a lot in investment costs is usually a prescription for mediocre returns.

14. It is hard to bolster your returns by picking superior stocks and stock funds. But it's easy to boost long-term performance by cutting back on bonds and money-market funds and increasing your portfolio's allocation to stocks.

15. Over the long haul, a mediocre stock fund will outperform a brilliant bond or money-fund manager.

16. A short-term bond will give you most of the yield of a long-term bond, but with a small fraction of the volatility.

17. When picking among bond and money market funds, your key criterion should be cost. If you stick with no-load funds with low annual expenses, you will almost always do better than in comparable funds with higher costs.

18. If you need cash, sell a stock-market loser rather than a winner. After all, you can't be sure which will perform better. But with the loser, at least you know the tax consequences will be pleasant, not painful.

19. For every $1 you pay in mortgage interest, you might save 28 cents in taxes (assuming you are in the 28 percent federal income-tax bracket). In other words, paying $1 of mortgage interest will leave you 72 cents poorer. The same brutal math applies to other vaunted tax deductions, such as those for making charitable gifts or paying state, local, and property taxes. The big exception to all this are tax-deductible retirement account contributions, because you save the 28 cents in taxes while still hanging onto your $1.

20. The easiest and cheapest way to cut your estate-tax bill is to give money away. Every year, for instance, both you and your spouse could give $10,000 to each of your three kids without triggering the gift tax. That would shrink your combined estate by $60,000.

21. Only insure against true disasters. If you have a young family to support, your death would be financially devastating, so you should have life insurance. But if your stereo dies, it wouldn't be a big deal, so you shouldn't pay for the extended warranty.

22. Remember, most of the long-term gain from owning a home comes from appreciation of the land. The house itself will tend to deteriorate, necessitating expensive repairs just to maintain its value. Indeed, partly because of this depreciation, you are unlikely to recoup the full cost of home improvements and repairs when you sell your house.

23. To avoid a big financial hit, steer clear of the derivatives market, don't bet heavily on any single stock and keep margin debt to a minimum.

24. Don't invest in a vacuum. If you are dutifully saving for a long and active retirement, it makes no sense to smoke, drink heavily, and never exercise.

25. When in doubt, do nothing. Leave your assets where they are until your course becomes clearer. It is almost always the cheapest course of action.

ETHICAL INVESTING

INVESTING ETHICALLY

Until the names Enron and WorldCom became infamous, socially responsible investing was hammered by critics for supposedly delivering below market returns. Investing articles would carry headlines like "Doing Good but Not So Well," suggesting that sub-par returns were the norm for companies with a conscience. Therefore, "green" investors and the proliferating number of socially oriented investment advisors were heartened when funds like the Parnassus Fund, one of the largest ethical funds, reported a five-year stellar return of 21.5 percent. This was a vindication of sorts for a segment of the investment industry that has long believed that ethics and profits need not be mutually exclusive.

"We've been tracking social investments for years," says Peter Kinder, president of Boston-based KLD, which devised the Domini Social Index to measure performance of socially screened stocks.

"It hasn't hurt investors to stay out of tobacco stocks or to load up on companies with good environmental or labor records. Just the opposite. Good business practices make good companies, not the other way around."

On the surface, ethical investing seems a no-brainer for anyone with a modicum of social conscience. "We won't invest in companies that sell tobacco products, or utility and mining firms that use nuclear power," explains David Shuttleworth, vice president of marketing and sales for the Ethical Funds, Canada's largest family of green mutual funds. These fund managers invest only in companies that can pass ethical screens that award high marks for good labor relations, generous charitable contributions, and a proactive environmental policy. They filter out firms that are involved in tobacco, alcohol, animal testing, or nuclear power.

Sin categories are the predominant social screen. There are compelling financial and ethical reasons to avoid tobacco stocks: The industry has reaped huge financial rewards by externalizing its societal costs, such as the health consequences of smoking, and it has consistently engaged in public relations subterfuge and marketing deceptions. The use of alcohol as a screen does not reflect the way most people in our society live. Unlike tobacco, alcohol does not carry with it an automatic stigma; some believe that, used in moderation, alcohol may have some beneficial side effects that are both psychological and physical.

Social screens may offer limited potential for modifying corporate behavior. But when combined with aggressive corporate governance, raising environmental reporting standards, and opening companies to more critical scrutiny of their social practices, changing consumer buying habits of products and of stocks can affect a company or industry's reputation and lead to significant reforms.

How important is ethical investing to you? This is a question only you can answer. As with all of your financial decisions, your lifestyle, values, and ethics will play a role in where you place your money, whether you realize it or not. Like most decisions, you want to feel good about making them, but you must realize that trade-offs are often inevitable.

CORPORATE DISHONESTY

Okay, we all remember that the raging bull market of the 1990s ended badly. Let's examine what we could have done better. Fed-

eral Chairman Alan Greenspan tried to tell us that we were participating in a bubble. He coined the term "irrational exuberance"
when talking about participation in the stock market. But even
Greenspan started to believe that some of that exuberance might
have been rational, after all. In 1997, just eight months after his
original warning, *Fortune* magazine said that Greenspan had gone
from taking away the punch bowl to spiking the punch. But regardless of who predicted what when, bull markets are bucking broncos,
and eventually they are going to leave anyone who tries to ride
them in the dust.

Anyone who invests in a company or a market that regularly
goes higher and higher (and higher) should expect some problems. I am a capitalist who believes in the long-term efficiency of the
free market. But that does not put me on the side of those who
think that everything is for the best in this best of all possible market economies.

Markets don't run on money; they run on trust. And trust
depends on the reliability and completeness of the information. I
enthusiastically endorse what Elliot Spitzer and the various groups
such as the SEC, NASD, and other State Attorney Generals did.
They went after the Wall Street analysts for failing to disclose their
conflicts of interest. Their firms were getting fees from the companies they were evaluating and—surprise!—companies that paid fees
tended to get more enthusiastic recommendations. No one really
would mind that practice except there was no way to tell which recommendations might have been influenced by financial ties. The
idea that everyone knew what was going on inside of Wall Street is
bogus. Sophisticated institutional investors who do their own
research might take analyst recommendations with a barrel of salt.
But retail investors who log on to Yahoo! just get a list of strong buy
recommendations without any context. They really had no way to
evaluate their objectivity.

The whole reason we have rules in place for public companies
is so that there will be enough checks and balances and enough
consequences to make sure that any natural human tendencies to
lie and steal are countered by incentives to prevent, catch, expose,
and minimize the lying and the stealing. If your daughter asks you
to invest in her lemonade stand, you can make a judgment based
on the invaluable information you already have about her trust-
worthiness and business judgment. But if you are going to invest in
someone you don't know, the system is supposed to make up for

your inability to get that kind of information. We limit public companies' liability and protect their privacy and liquidity. We make them tell you a lot about their business, and just to make sure they are telling the truth, we bring in some outsiders—auditors and boards of directors—to double check. We need to make sure that the incentives we have in place make it clear to corporate managers, directors, and auditors, who are supposed to be so good at cost-benefit analysis, that it is not worth it to try to lie. Yes, there will always be people who will commit fraud anyway, but when it rises to the level that it did that year, we need to take another look at the systems we have for prevention and punishment. Perhaps they need to be recalibrated.

There were a lot of low points in corporate trust, but the lowest had to be these: First, the fact that the Enron board of directors waived the conflict-of-interest rules so that the CFO could enter into the special-purpose entity deals that brought the company down. Second was Arthur Andersen's approval of WorldCom's switching of billions of dollars of expenses from operating to capital, just in time to support an enormous debt offering. And third, when Deutsche Asset Management voted its Hewlett-Packard shares against the merger with Compaq, the managers got a call from their investment banking side, asking them to meet with HP executives. After the meeting—and a new million-dollar fee—DAM switched its vote.

We need to count on the board of directors, the auditors, the analysts, or the shareholders to recognize, prevent, or respond to management abuses, otherwise Wall Street won't work and we should invest our money in tulips or dot.com stocks.

DISHONESTY, GREED, AND HYPOCRISY IN CORPORATE AMERICA

The Year 2000 brought hard times for Wall Street, the American economy, and President George W. Bush. As the conservative and pro-business major publication *Fortune* reported, ongoing revelations of corporate wrongdoing and accounting scandals "created a crisis of investor confidence the likes of which hasn't been seen since the Great Depression."

The bad news began with Enron, the largest corporate bankruptcy in American history. Enron executives, propelled by greed, were not satisfied with immense salaries: They set up all sorts of spin-off partnerships to enrich themselves at the expense of stock-holders and the corporation's bottom line. In a little more than a decade, Enron soared from obscurity to become the nation's seventh largest company, with over 20,000 employees in 40 countries. But its dishonesty about profits and its off-the-books energy deals, abetted by fiscal accounting that was erroneous, misleading, and downright dishonest, eventually caused an implosion of gigantic proportions.

On December 28, 2000, Enron stock sold at over $84 a share. Eleven months later to the day, Enron shares plummeted to less than a dollar in the heaviest trading volume in a corporation ever recorded by a major stock exchange. The investors in the company—many of them Enron employees—rushed to get out of the stock before it became totally worthless. Two months later Enron stock was delisted by the New York Stock Exchange, and today its stock is just that, worthless. The federal Justice Department is in the midst of a criminal investigation of the energy-trading company, but the damage to shareholders and pensioners has already been done.

Enron was just the beginning, as example after example of corporate greed and accounting malfeasance has come to light. Every one of the corporations I shall discuss is—or was at one time—among America's largest companies.

The regional telephone company Qwest provided basic telephone service to 14 states, had revenues of over $18 billion a year, and handled 240 million phone calls and 600 million e-mails each day before they ran astray. The fourth largest U.S. telephone company, Qwest came under federal investigation for criminal corporate practices. The Securities and Exchange Commission (SEC) had to examine its accounting procedures. These indications of likely fiscal impropriety caused its stock to crash from its high of $67 two years ago to just under $2, before it started repairing its image and credibility.

Tyco International is one of the world's largest conglomerates, operating in over 80 countries with revenues of over $36 billion. Huge questions surfaced about the way in which the corporation accounted for the multiple acquisitions that transformed it from a small company into a corporate behemoth. Its CEO, Dennis Kozlowski, was forced to resign, and shortly afterwards was arraigned on charges of tax evasion. Tyco, which sold at $60 a share, in the wake of the financial irregularities in its booking of acquisitions, fell to just over $10 a share. After Kozlowski was arrested, the stock began to recover.

Compared to Adelphia Communications, one of America's largest cable television providers, Tyco performed well on the stock market during the scandal. According to *Business Week*, Adelphia was valued at between $9.5 billion and $11.8 billion. That was before Adelphia entered bankruptcy following disclosures that its finances were in disarray, in large measure because it had made $2.3 billion in off-balance-sheet loans to partnerships run by the family of John Rigas, the CEO of Adelphia. Its bankruptcy is the fifth largest such filing since 1980. Adelphia's shares sold for $42 dollars a year ago but as of this writing, they had dropped to $.70 and all trading of the shares has been halted.

Global Crossing, which had a major role in the development of fiber optic cable networks, is under investigation by the SEC for fraudulent accounting. The corporation, it appears, arranged "deals" in which no goods or services were exchanged, but which nonetheless made it appear that profit was being generated. These purely paper transactions inflated the company's revenue substantially. Global Crossing also filed for bankruptcy. Its share price was over $60 and when the scandal hit, the shares fell 99.9 percent before finally becoming worthless.

American stock markets (and world markets) were shaken by the demise of WorldCom. Its balance sheet listed assets of $103 billion and net income of over $1 billion. Yet it was revealed that fraudulent accounting hid $3.8 billion in losses, and that additional losses were forthcoming. What this huge telecommunications company did was record daily costs as capital expenditures, a dishonest procedure that allowed it to erase enormous operating losses and record a sizeable but illusory profit. At one point, WorldCom stock traded at $64, only to see shares of the company plummet to nothing. It defaulted on over $4.25 billion of its obligations.

It might seem that things could not get any dirtier, yet they can. To add to the chronicle of greed and dishonesty just cited, there is the matter of hypocrisy. The hypocrisy is of significant importance to the developing world, which, incidentally, is the major victim of that hypocrisy.

The International Monetary Fund (IMF) functions as a sort of global economic police officer, requiring countries that seek loans to get their fiscal house in order as a precondition to economic assistance. One of the chief demands of the IMF is transparency. For markets to work and for the appropriate signals for efficient resource allocation to be provided, investors must have as much information as possible. Investors need assurance that the information received adequately reflects the economic situation of a firm. But such assurance has not been forthcoming in the United States. Instead, corporations have cooked their books, hiding their debt and artificially inflating profit. They have even, as in the case of WorldCom, falsified EBITDA (Earnings Before Interest, Taxes, Depreciation, and Amortization), the major measure of earnings flow, previously deemed beyond manipulation. Individual investors, pension funds, and mutual shares funds all are demanding honesty and openness in corporate accounting. They want transparency.

But a great number of corporate executives do not want changes that would compel transparency and severely penalize those who circumvent the honest reporting of financial data. They want to be able to report profits, whether their corporation actually has generated them or not, so their tenure remains secure. They want their corporations to loan them money. They want huge bundles of stock options without accounting for those options as a corporate expense. They want to manipulate stock prices, so that they can reap windfall profits from these options.

One could call it greed. Or dishonesty. Or hypocrisy. Whatever it is, it has been running rampant in the executive suites of government and business in America.

MY CLOSING TWO CENTS

This book is about education. It is a primer to help get your finances on track, using all of the tools at your disposal. Reading this book is the easy part. Doing the homework, reading the annual reports, talking to professionals, and taking the fear out of your financial life: That's the hard part.

Personal finance isn't a hobby, it's a chore. So do yours. Earn. Learn. Save. Invest.

Index

193

About the Authors

Robert Black *Television, Radio, Multimedia, and Money Manager* Best known for his stock analysis and "Generation-X" approach, Rob Black has helped investors correctly manage their money for over a decade. Rob lives and breathes money. Currently, he serves as investment strategist for GLB Wealth Management, a global money management firm serving prestigious institutions and high net worth individuals. Rob is a widely published author and market commentator; his expertise is featured in prominent finance and business publications, as well as other professional media outlets. He began his career in media over ten years ago as a business correspondent for Business Talk Radio. On the nationally syndicated show *Stock Talk*, Rob presented the stories behind the stories on Wall Street, and explained why stocks moved higher or lower. *Stock Talk* was the highest-rated show ever on CNET Radio and delivered a 600% increase in listeners. Rob donates nearly 100% of his media compensation to local and national branches of the Children's Hospital, and he lives in San Francisco, California.

Pam Krueger *Executive Producer/Anchor and Veteran Financial Anchor/ Reporter* As the coanchor of PBS's *MoneyTrack* and former coanchor and producer of TechTV's, *The Money Machine*, Pam Krueger has been imparting financial wisdom to viewers for ten years. Pam is also a regularly featured money reporter for the Emmy Winning show, *Money Moves*, seen on PBS. In 2001, she produced *NETworth*, a one-hour special that was broadcast on more than 70 PBS stations. Pam has a passion for economics and has been a stockbroker for nine years.